This is a personal account of the significant journey of one naïve teenager, undertaking his two years of National Service in the Royal Artillery, from leaving school to serving in the almost-forgotten and little-understood United Nations Korean War.

*To Stephen & Carolyn
With best wishes
Peter, Oct 2019.*

To Mary and Neil, who first taught me that in respecting others, one must respect and be true to oneself; and to Margaret, who constantly reminds me.

Peter Hutchinson

7287

Called Up – A Journey to the Korean War

AUSTIN MACAULEY PUBLISHERS™
LONDON · CAMBRIDGE · NEW YORK · SHARJAH

Copyright © Peter Hutchinson (2019)

The right of Peter Hutchinson to be identified as author of this work has been asserted by him in accordance with section 77 and 78 of the Copyright, Designs and Patents Act 1988.

All rights reserved. No part of this publication may be reproduced, stored in a retrieval system, or transmitted in any form or by any means, electronic, mechanical, photocopying, recording, or otherwise, without the prior permission of the publishers.

Any person who commits any unauthorised act in relation to this publication may be liable to criminal prosecution and civil claims for damages.

A CIP catalogue record for this title is available from the British Library.

ISBN 9781786937964 (Paperback)
ISBN 9781786937971 (Hardback)
ISBN 9781528952194 (ePub e-book)

www.austinmacauley.com

First Published (2019)
Austin Macauley Publishers Ltd
25 Canada Square
Canary Wharf
London
E14 5LQ

*"Every event and indeed every word and action in the external world remain unintelligible as far as we are concerned if they do not reveal to us that which speaks and acts within, and if there is no clue to their meaning in the inmost depths of the spirit. There can be revealed to us only that which is revealed **in** us, for only that which happens within can have any meaning for us."*

Berdyaev N, 'Freedom and the Spirit' p.93

Contents

1.	Paddling in Deep Water	11
2.	Swimming with the Stream	20
3.	Syncopated Swimming	34
4.	Can You Really Swim Well?	37
5.	Starting to Get Somewhere	41
6.	Floating	53
7.	A Reflective Interlude	58
8.	Momentary Passing Glory	63
9.	Indecision – Going or Staying?	66
10.	Sailing – Discovering the World	69
11.	Why a Korean War?	73
12.	Japan	81
13.	Finally – Korea	90
14.	What Is an Air Op Flight?	94
15.	Daily Life by the Imjin River	99
16.	Living Accommodation	102
17.	Chief Clerk	108
18.	Food	113
19.	The Church and Its Chaplains	119
20.	Rest and Recuperation	124

21. A New CO	128
22. Coming Home	133
Postscript	135

1. Paddling in Deep Water

It might be expected that any youngster, setting off on an unknown journey into what can only be called an experiment, might have been somewhat tense and showing stress by the usual or common ways such as biting my nails, wringing my hands or showing other obvious signs of tension and anxiety. In fact, having just said goodbye to my father, mother and sister, I had some emotional feelings about that but still sat in the train carriage quite calm and apparently unconcerned. I have often reflected since on how it came to be that I could be so cool and collected, and it comes, I feel, from my family's history and the way in which I had been brought up. That seems a good place to start this story.

For one quite obvious matter is that, compared to most children, throughout my life I had regularly been on the move. I was born in Kent, though Mum and Dad were Northerners, she born and bred in Shildon, County Durham, Dad born in Westmorland (as it was then, Cumbria as it is now) though his family moved to Shildon when he was only a small child, because it was the site of a major railway works and Grandpa was a railway guard. Our homes in the eight years I was in Kent were rented houses and so we moved from house to house as opportunity offered or necessity demanded. Dad's base was in the village of Aylesham, and I think we had three homes in the village at different times. Other times we lived in neighbouring villages and once in Deal. It also meant that I had two primary schools, for my first was a long walk for myself and the other village children to get to school. It was also a long cycle ride for my father to get to work in Aylesham. Once we left Kent and moved to Sheffield, for the 1st of September 1939, also the start of the war, there was a move after a year bringing, for us, two homes and for me two schools and sets of friends. Then at 11 there came the further move to grammar school, for two years, before we moved on again to spend three years in my middle grammar school. One further move brought me to my third grammar school for my time in the 6th Form.

Thus, change had been an integral part of my life and, without all the current modern technology that facilitates people keeping in touch with each other, this meant a complete break with friends and fresh starts at making new ones. As a newcomer, I was not always welcomed and can still recall, as if it were yesterday, following the Sheffield headmaster into the classroom I was to join and, as we walked down the aisle, between the desks, to the teacher's desk, the form bully muttered something like,

"Who's this? We'll get him at play time."

It was only a whisper but I heard it loud and clear, as I was intended to! He was much bigger and stronger than me, and bore the confidence of his father, who was a manager in a local steel works, and he expected all to be beholden to him as king of the school. Most of us kept out of his way. In the world of adults and local authority educational planning, children's relationships seemed to count for nothing, but the reality was different, and not always simple or pleasant. When we left Sheffield, I was allocated a place in a West Riding grammar school in Ecclesfield until, a few days before term started, we received a missive changing this and informing my parents that I had to report to Barnsley Holgate Grammar School. Not much of a change, one might think, except that I was the only child from our village who travelled to Barnsley to go to an all-boys school. No other boy in the school came from anywhere near my neck of the woods and I made no real friends there. Also, clearly, I was isolated among my peers in the village I lived in, many of whom did not go to the grammar school, but the boys and girls who did, went to the school I thought I was to attend. I never knew any of the incidents that made up the gossip among them, knew none of the school staff's names or habits and whether liked or not, and whether they were thought good or not.

Without further labouring the point, I had faced change again and again and had little expectation of it, other than it had to be endured and usually it wasn't too bad. It simply was a fact of life that, for me, had to be managed as best as I could. The way life was arranged featured quite plainly in our family life and indeed in the wider circles in which I moved. This was largely because children hardly figured in the decisions that were taken about us by employers or authorities. I am sure that my parents always had my best interests at heart and tried to manage our moves so that they were at the best time for me and my schooling, but they only had a very limited control of such matters.

If I expand that comment to include the wider society in which I was brought up, then the same situation largely applied there too. During and since the First World War there seems to have been an expectation of considerable change from the Victorian, almost feudal, configuration of power, authority and wealth in Britain. In fact, even by the Second World War, little had changed, especially in the mining villages in which I had lived all my life. I never went down a pit but soon learned that they were dangerous places where death was a frequent visitor. As Dad ran the drapers shop in Aylesham, he, and thus we as a family, knew of every accident and mishap that took place, for the local doctor would have called into the shop,

"Can I have a reel of black cotton?"

"Oh dear, that sounds as if there's been an accident?"

Dad would reply.

"Yes."

And then whatever details he had been given would, in general, be passed on, and almost certainly before the shop closed whatever information there was would be passed on in terms of the number killed or maimed and in hospital, and which families had been affected. Such 'accidents', however minor, were significant for the families involved for not only was there the personal pain in death or changed circumstances but the financial consequences were severe with the loss of a wage, no sickness pay or benefit, and doctor's bills to pay. Poor housing, poverty and insecurity was the norm of the communities in which I lived and moved, and all were beholden to those in authority, usually the very rich and powerful.

Slowly through my childhood I gathered something of my parents' history and how the times through which they lived had impacted upon them. Mother left school at 13 or 14 and, as the youngest of eight children, stayed at home to help my Grandmother. Dad similarly left school at the same age, unable to obtain the scholarship he expected, and was clearly capable of gaining, because at the time of the examination he was not at school because he had scarlet fever. He'd missed his chance and it didn't arise again! I have since discovered how such things were common in the northern working class areas of the country and how the majority of the people had few opportunities but suffered and faced little real change in their lives. Whatever talk or expectations there were in the 1914–18 era, little changed for the few men who returned and were fit or able enough to resume their working life. The mines were owned by the aristocrats in whose lands the mineral rights resided. As owners, they continued to live in their grand houses, supported by many servants, whose hard life and poor working conditions were accepted because it was a better life than any alternative available. Boys started working in the pits at 13 years of age, facing, at that age, a transition into manhood for they were then part of the family's financial support. Their initiation was frightening for they were often, having been 'initiated' by their fellow boy miners, taken by the Overseer to their place of work and left alone in the all-encompassing darkness, a darkness that all witnesses say is so complete as to out-compete any other darkness. The underground pit roadway might be no more than inches high or wide, roughhewn and strewn with rubble and rocks. Great care had to be taken to maintain and manage one's lamp, for it was the only glimmer of light the boy would have, and it would have been so easy not to trim the wick correctly, to knock the lamp over or fail to shield it from the draughts of air that were necessary to life, but would blow out the light in an instant. All miners' families knew the reality of financial hardship for they were housed in terraced houses built by the colliery owners, without indoor sanitation or water.[1] They were subject to the owner's whims as to when they worked, for roof falls, bad air, flooding and the like would all require a cessation of work and if the men did not work they were not paid, often for days even weeks. When accidents struck, which they did frequently, many had little support from the owners and were evicted from their homes and were not given a pension or financial support.

How my parents came to be in Kent was unusual, though not entirely out of the ordinary. It happened because in 1926, before their marriage, my father went on strike about some new conditions being imposed by the Co-operative Society for which he worked. Although he was personally unaffected, he went, with the majority, on strike, as, for him, it was a matter of principle. The staff's complaint was never resolved, other than by the senior managers offering promotion or better conditions to selected staff in order to persuade them to return to work, and many did. Dad couldn't accept such a way of sorting out the problem so his only option was to leave, which he did. He found another job in Leeds, miles from his Durham home. The implications for him and Mum, as a courting couple, they never mentioned, but with him having to lodge in Leeds and return home each weekend, courting must have strained the budget, as well as their relationship.

---

[1] For a vivid description of actual living conditions, see G. Orwell's *Road to Wigan Pier*.

In those days, grocery shops were open for very long hours so their opportunity for meeting must have been extremely limited. Even before the strike, when Dad managed a shop in Spennymoor but was the only member of staff, the shop was open until 11 pm on a Saturday night and the whole raison d'être of the retail trade was that the customer was always right and, in all circumstances, to be served with a smile. If one regular incident that he told me about was typical, serving with a smile must have been very difficult. The bus to get him home to Shildon left at 11:03 pm so, as customers thinned out late in the evening, he would have everything cleaned and stored away at the coolest part of the premises, for there were no freezers then, ready to run for the bus. One customer regularly appeared at 10:55pm and always requested cheese, kept in the coolest part of the building right at the back, and already put away. By the time he was served Dad would miss the bus and face a seven mile, two hour walk home. If that was the common life for grocery staff, working in Leeds must have severely limited my parents' opportunities of being together at all.

The above is a small snapshot of my father's harsh working life in the 1920s, but this seems to be minor compared to the conditions under which miners and those in steel foundries or other large factories existed. Under the leadership of the miners, matters figuratively 'came to a head' in 1926 when there was a general strike involving almost all working men. They simply wanted better conditions; a wage sufficient to live on in some comfort rather than a bare existence; continuous work rather than the constant week-on, week-off or similar short time practices that were common and allied to the no-work-no-pay conditions that were almost universal; working conditions that were safer and support, with financial help, when accidents, causing injuries or death, happened. Unfortunately, these straightforward humane demands were not seen as such by either the government or the rich owners. Their minds were filled with the events in Russia, with its socialist philosophy and its communist propaganda and conditions. They saw the general strike as a revolution in the making and took the necessary steps to ensure that the 'state' continued and the 'revolution' was defeated. So, the police and some soldiers were used to quell demonstrations, often called riots, and to keep order.[2]

So, when Mum and he married, one of his friends, who had already decamped to seaside Deal in Kent and opened a drapers shop, asked Dad to join him in the business, enabling a second shop in Aylesham to be opened. The Kent coalfield had recently started up and, with many Welsh miners moving in, there was a good business opportunity. Housing was not provided so it necessitated them renting homes as close to the Aylesham shop as possible. Hence in my eight years there, we moved as many times as my years!

One of the interesting facts of these events, as far as they impacted on me, was that, whilst I knew of Dad's involvement in the strike, the reasons for it and the rationale for his refusing to return to work for the Co-operative Society, nothing was ever said to me, by either parent, about the wider conditions and the concerns that led to a national and general strike. I have no idea how that influenced Mum and Dad in their marrying or their move to Kent. It seems as if they could get angry and react strongly to their own situation, but still, deep down, accept the overall conditions for what, in reality, they were – matters that, as individuals, neither they nor other working folk could change or do little about. My father had feelings about such things but only rarely did he express anything of what they were. One small example came when, in 1948, as a family we paid a return visit to see old friends in Kent. There for his first few months Dad had lodged, in an agricultural village, with a couple, where the man was a skilled craftsman, but only doing odd jobs, keeping and living off his garden. Dad thought the world of him and, as we walked through that magnificent garden, they recalled that, whilst average wages were £1 or £2 a week, others were getting more. One phrase Dad used was,

---

[2] For a fuller description of the general strike and government documents see *Black Diamonds: The Rise and Fall of an English Dynasty* by Catherine Bailey.

"Yes, but the Rector was paid £1,000 a year, even in those days."

Thus, changes and new experiences had been regular occurrences for me throughout my first 19 years and I had learned to put up with them, the upheaval and practical turmoil, seemingly largely unmoved and without registering much, if any, emotion. The mould I had been brought up in was one of acceptance of the status quo, carrying on whatever the hardship or conditions, and saying little or nothing. Nor was there much point in exploring the reasons for things as they were or questioning why they were that way. In my grammar school 6th Form, four of us studied economics, social history and the British constitution in the then South East Essex Technical College with a group of ex-soldiers, among others, who were going on to the London School of Economics (LSE), and I studied these as academic matters without considering their impact on us. Out of the whole 6th Form group, only one was really interested in politics, and he was an active Labour party supporter, committed and canvassing to achieve social change. He was something of an oddity and his passion influenced me not at all, at that time!

In 1939, my dad became a Lay Pastor in the Methodist Church, later a full Methodist minister, and once, years later, he explained that,

"Sadly, I heard the call from God but put off that step for 14 years before I answered it."

Contemplating that circumstance when, in 1925, he heard what he felt was a call from God to candidate for the ministry of the church, I wonder just what was going on for him then and in the immediate years that followed. At 24, he was a Fellow of the Grocers Society; managing a single person shop for the Co-operative Society; in love and courting the love of his life, Mum; when the majority of his then world were preparing and fighting for a better world in a general strike, he participated in a strike, lost his job, moved away to Leeds and ended up in Kent. So keeping to himself, and doing nothing about a sense of God's calling to the ministry of the church, may well have seemed the only option available. I am so aware of a man who kept his heart, the well spring of his life, his view of the world and his life within it, well hidden. That was the mould into which I was poured.

2. Swimming with the Stream

So now I sat on the Paddington to Holyhead mainline express train for the short journey to the tiny Welsh border town of Gobowen, my call up papers safely in my case, to begin the next completely new experience, National Service. In one sense, it is unsurprising that I was outwardly unperturbed about something that had been a part of my, and every other British young man's, expectations for the past two years.

Effectively from the start of the second world war in September 1939, all men aged 18 to 41 were liable to be conscripted for 'war service' unless they were medically unfit or working in certain 'reserved' occupations that were recognised as being vital to the war effort. By 1942, the upper age limit for men was raised to 51 years and women between 20 and 30 years were also liable to be called up. For men, there were some exclusions such as those resident in Northern Ireland, students, clergy, and anyone blind or with a mental disorder. Once the war ended in 1945 two distinct processes happened. First, men who were urgently needed for the recovery process, such as those in the building trades, were released as soon as practical. Then serving soldiers were given phased release dates according to their age and length of service, and this release of serving wartime conscripts continued until 1949.

The rules changed at the end of the war in 1945, but peacetime conscription was regularised in the National Service Act of 1948 that came into force in January 1949 and required all males between the ages of 17 and 21 to serve in the armed forces, for 18 months, and who were then kept on the reserve list for a further four years. During those four years, men could be recalled to their units for up to 20 days, on no more than three occasions, for continued training. Those deemed to be in essential services were exempt for a period of eight years unless they left the essential service. There was a further change in October 1950, a month after I commenced my service, when the period of service was extended by six months to two years, though the period on the reserve list was reduced by the same amount. Although the detail never seemed to be clear in the public mind, the wartime exemptions were continued.

What was well known, by those youngsters with 'street cred', was that, although it was acceptable for those thought suitable to become officers, there were limits to the jobs a national serviceman could undertake. The general view seemed to be that there were better opportunities for interesting work in the RAF. Many of the best informed also knew that it was possible to sign up for a three-year period of service, during which one was thought of and dealt with as a 'regular', which increased the pay one received and also meant one was paid for the three years one spent on the reserve list. For some this was a significantly better option, especially if one hadn't already obtained a secure working future, and was thus chosen by them. For instance, if one wanted to fly in the RAF, it was much better to be on a three-year regular service than a national serviceman.

If I am anything like the common or ordinary crowd, there must have been something in our understanding of our national life that enabled us to accept national service in the armed forces as a norm. I have no recollection, although I was in the 6th Form at school when national service was re-introduced, of feeling aggrieved or distressed or indeed having any strong feelings about it. It was something we would all have to do so we might as well get on with it. Clearly some lads' fathers were assiduous in guiding them through the few choices we had to make. As an example, my best friend, a very active and promising musician, chose to go into the RAF, though he had no real idea why. It was his father's advice! It worked well for him, in that he, as an Essex boy, spent his entire two years based in London, with its regular musical events, invaluable for a musician.

So, only 18 months later, the length of service already increased to two years, what had been a fact of life for as long as I could remember was now becoming a reality. The whole of my family upbringing had taught me that there was no point in having any feelings about life's events, such as this, at all. Things happen in life, such as illnesses or moving house, going to new schools, taking examinations – all sorts of different experiences happen both pleasant and unpleasant, rewarding and satisfying or quite the reverse. There were also other things that one desired, wanted, even longed for but could not be obtained because there was some sound reason, such as 'we can't afford it', and that was that! All such matters were things about which nothing could be done – so it was best simply to get on with them and make the best one could of the situation. So now this 'National Service' was another in the same category – it was now happening, and there was nothing that I could do about it!

But I couldn't help wondering how I had come to be going to a Royal Artillery camp and just what that would mean. There had been opportunity to express a preference on some of the papers that I had been required to fill in long ago, and some of my friends had had very clear ideas of what they wanted. My best friend, Keith, was one of those who wanted to go into the RAF and was even now on his way to some camp to begin his training. Other friends had very firm desires to join one or other service but had not achieved what they wanted. To some, who had wanted to serve in the same service as father, older brother or other close relative, it was a matter of deep anger, for they felt their preference had counted for nothing. Some I knew had chosen because they thought it would be an easier option or would give them a greater chance of training in a field that would help when they returned to civilian life again. None of these things seemed to have counted for much for the vast majority who, on the whole, like me, shrugged their shoulders and got on with what had to be done. Not that I had any preference at all, for none of my relatives had, to my then knowledge, ever served in any fighting service. Nor had many in my world ever been able to choose exactly what they wanted to do as and when they wanted. Such freedom hadn't figured much in my experience so far.

I sat and took in the attractive but unfamiliar Shropshire scenery until the train arrived at Gobowen station. I'd never heard of it before and it seemed to be little more than a station platform! Once the train had steamed on its way, towards Holyhead, it was a surprise to see just how many young men, like myself, had left the train. Sitting in the carriage for the two-station journey I had taken, I hadn't seen another youngster like myself and now, standing on the platform, there seemed to be hundreds. This was a regular fortnightly arrival of National Service Trainees and was clearly a routine that was well organised. As we moved towards the gates, Sergeants with clipboards containing lists of names, stood and, having checked with his list, simply said,

"NAME?"

and, hearing the response, instructed,

"Stand there,"

or,

"Go over there to that line."

Everyone was dealt with in exactly the same way, and relatively quickly we were marshalled by these three-stripe carrying Sergeants, with their lists of names, and eventually everyone was marshalled on to coaches.

The three-mile journey took little time and we were soon given our first view of the Oswestry Royal Artillery initial training camp, located at Park Hall, some two and a half miles from the town. Under the control of the ubiquitous 'Sergeants' the processing began, and the process might easily be viewed as the very efficient, sorting out of a large group of uncertain youngsters. This is the sort of thing the army does very well. Alternatively, it might be viewed as a process of losing one's identity to become simply one small cog in a very large machine. Being the sort of person I was, I simply accepted it as the former model and only later came to see a different picture.

Thus the process began with the checking of names, and I was given my unalterable, never to be forgotten army number 22407287, by which I was to be known hereafter; my service record and pay book, known as the AB 64; the army identity tag, to be worn round my neck at all times. We were also given a standard printed letter to report my safe arrival, and brown paper and string to make a parcel of my civilian clothes to return them home. It was already clear that we had been divided into groups of around 20 and were soon told that as a group we 'belonged' to a particular Sergeant who was to be obeyed fully and instantly at all times,

"Or there'll be trouble!"[3]

Having now become 7287, the next thing was to lose any sense of personality and become one of the amorphous Royal Artillery gunners, joining all the others who were already 'uniformed'. We had to get kitted out. Each Sergeant's group was formed up in threes and marched in turn to the Quartermaster Sergeant's store. The British pastime of queueing was very much alive and well, though there wasn't much time wasted! In turn, each group approached a sort of counter, for me reminiscent of those on either side of the drapers store Dad had run when I was a small boy in Kent, and one of the soldiers behind it would take a look, and usually without so much as a word, would offer a pile of khaki army clothes that he considered would fit. Occasionally there would be a break, as some extra tall or short, large or small individual would be asked if he knew his size, and every now

---

[3] See a similar account of *67 Oswestry training Regiment* by John Flann (1949)

and then, a tape measure would be put round a chest, or a height demanded, before that person became the recipient of his pile of clothing. For me, kitting out was relatively easy, for my ex-draper Dad had always told me that I was 'stock size', to use one of his phrases. This speedy and quite brutal system usually, but not always, worked well, for the selected garments were not always guaranteed to fit. As we were instructed to try on the blouse type jackets, there were soon some complaints about the fit. The Sergeant or other soldier would do a hasty check with trousers held against the waist, or a manipulation, or even a try on of the jacket would follow. Out of which only the most obviously incorrect ones – such as trousers too long or short, or an incorrect chest size – would lead to a change. Others were brushed aside as being of little significance. It was a matter of constant surprise, in the weeks that followed, to find that we did all look 'uniform' and reasonably smart.

Only when we came to the boots was there any individual selection. There were piles of boots, tied by a piece of string into pairs, on the floor and we new recruits were told to choose two pairs that fit us. There were stern warnings that a deal of time would be spent in boots and all must make sure they got the fit right, because the boots would not, under any circumstances, be changed. There were some brown boots among the piles and it was pointed out that these were officers' boots.

"And if you're a namby-pamby who fancies a pair, then you'll also be a bloody idiot! The first thing you'll have to do is to make them lovely brown boots BLACK and you'll have to keep 'em that way,"

This was the Sergeant's warning.

"And anyway, you can't have more than one pair of brown."

It was a firm and precise instruction. After trying on a few pairs, it was quite clear to me that the fit, comfort and general standard of the brown boots were of much better quality, and, although the downside was that the boots would have to be died black and kept in that condition, I decided it was worth the gamble to try to have two pairs. When the inevitable challenge followed, I disarmingly explained,

"But, sir, none of the black ones that are left fit me."

By this time, I was also about the last person still remaining in the QM's store and, no doubt, another group would be ready to come in and be fitted out so, with a warning that the consequence was on my own head, I was allowed to keep both pairs of brown boots! On balance, it worked out well, for getting them into acceptable condition was not a one sided chore. As well as all the boots having to be black, they also had to have their toe caps polished to a high shine, and, as the black leather was coarse and uneven, it necessitated smoothing the toe cap. This was normally achieved by working with something like a tooth brush handle, warmed in hot water, to smooth over the offending toe caps. It took a great deal of spit and polish and hard work over the ensuing few evenings. Dealing with our boots took everyone the best part of, at least, a couple of evenings! Some, of course, failed to make the grade when next examined by Sergeant, and the offender was told to get his boots up to the grade by the next day – another night spitting and rubbing, and using even more elbow grease. I found that getting the whole of my brown boots dyed black took no longer, and shining the smooth leather was a lot easier than achieving the same result on the coarser black leather. Nor did I ever have any complaint from Sergeant!

The accommodation, to which we were then shown, was in long Nissen type huts, with a row of beds down each side. The last thing, before we finally left the QM's store, was to be given, and made to carry, our bedding, consisting of a pillow, sheets and blankets, even though we were now to 'march', for we were no longer to walk anywhere but to march. As a group, we were marched in to 'our' hut and allocated a bed on to which our bedding had to be placed. We soon discovered that the only bit of private space we would have was the allotted bed and locker, but that did not avoid instructions as to the correct way to fold our sheets. We were told that we would always be responsible for making our beds and, once we had got out of bed each morning, the sheets and blankets were to be folded in the specified manner and placed, all folded exactly the same, at the bottom of our beds. The beds, with their bedding conveniently placed to be seen, and we ourselves would be inspected every morning. The dire warning was the unspecified threat,

"Woe betide anyone who doesn't do it right."

Exacting standards had just been explained without any reason for them being offered, and this was the way things worked in what was our new world and way of life!

There was a little time left before our next chore and we were simply told that our clothes were to be packed and sent home, and any personal articles were to be hidden away in the bedside lockers in a neat and tidy fashion. Later on, we were to discover that these too could be inspected and, if not neat and tidy, would be the subject of a bitter tirade that might question the nature of the upbringing that had obviously been our unfortunate lot.

Once the time allowed for sorting out one's bed space was over, we were taken out lined up in threes and marched to the dining hall. Our first meal was queued for and served in much the same way as the clothes had been distributed. There was enough food, but little choice and no discussion of likes or dislikes. If there was a choice, we selected the one wanted. In any other circumstance,

"Do you want it or not?"

was the only option available. It was a largely silent meal for there had not even been time or opportunity to gather much beyond each other's names, for they were not used by

Sergeant in marshalling and instructing us. Likewise, his comments had already begun to show what his sense of the character of each one of us was. Whether his judgement was anything like correct we would all find out in succeeding days!

Once the meal was over we might have assumed that we would be free! But with the mass of instructions already given to be completed, the sorting out of equipment and its cleaning, as well as the necessary and immediate work on boots, there was little time for anyone to do more than begin to find out the basic facts about neighbours, who were to become one's closest associates for the next six weeks, and possibly longer.

The largest shock was left until the next morning when, at an hour many had not known existed before, the hut door was thrown open with a stamping of boots as the Sergeant marched down the central aisle, banging each bed with his stick or homemade cudgel, and shouting in his extremely loud and raucous voice,

"Come on, you lazy good for nothings, out you get and stand by your beds, NOW."

Any reluctance would be dealt with immediately, in the now usual way, with a 'bollocking' or verbal tirade!

"What's the matter with you? Still tired, are we? Expecting Mummy to come with a cup of tea, are we? Well, you won't get one from me. Get your bloody feet on this deck NOW."

Any reluctant waker would be stood over, whilst the bellowing continued, until we all stood at attention at the bottom of our beds. Later mornings would reveal the essential characters not just of Sergeant, but also Bombardiers with their one or two stripes and even, very occasionally, of the Subaltern in charge, as each performed this ritual with greater or lesser shouting, stamping of feet, banging of beds, as well as the choice of language – the richness of 'swear words' employed was very revealing.

In the succeeding days with their regimented pattern, the first and most important matter to be dealt with was to ensure that we young incomplete recruits understood the nature of our situation. It was made clear, in different ways, but first by explanation in the classroom or more raucously on the parade ground, the true nature of our national service. Recruits serving their national service were part of the King's army, and as such had given all their rights, and not a few responsibilities, to the sovereign. Work would be allocated to us and if it were for 24 hours a day, and seven days a week, well, so be it. We would not be paid as a right; but out of the kindness of their heart, the army had accepted that seven shillings (35p) a week would be allowed for personal expenses.

If we youngsters had the temerity to be thinking and wanting to ask about when we would get our first leave, the answer was clear,

"There is no right to leave. What do you think this is, Butlins? If you're wanted here, you'll be here. And I'll b... well be here to make sure you good for nothings are doing what you have to."

However, assuming that our behaviour was good, all work had been duly completed and the relevant, unspecified standard achieved, time off in an evening and even leave might be granted. In the case of our Sergeant, he made it clear that, irrespective of all the work done and good behaviour, leave would largely depend on the gracious kindness of the Sergeant in whose gift this matter, as most others, apparently resided.

In case there were some who were unsure of themselves or unable quite to comprehend or indeed foolish enough to consider that such matters might be changed even altered, there were many occasions on which the message could be made quite clear. One false step or a moment's lack of concentration when marching, and there was much marching in these first weeks, would inevitably require Sergeant to shout his loudest at the offender, and in the process, include all others who had so far not managed to backslide, that, without his say,

"You won't get no leave," or, "I'll keep you b...rs here all night if I have to, until you get it right," or, "On my watch, if you think you can turn up looking like that, I'll see that you never…"

Due respect was to be given at all times to officers and sergeants on the basis that they were the King's representatives, who held absolute command and authority over the scum they had been given to rule over. The reality of this was forcefully brought home to me on one occasion, some weeks into the training, as I was walking, on my own, from one place to another that necessitated my crossing a corner of one of the two vast 'squares' that were co-terminus at that corner. Without seeing anyone in the other square, my lack of concentration was shattered by a high pitched piercing cry from the farthest corner of that square, ordering me to,

"Come here, boy!"

rapidly followed by the usual and forceful cry,

"At the double."

I responded and arrived to stand before the officer, who I knew to be the adjutant of the training camp, to be severely reprimanded because I had not saluted this self-same representative of His Majesty. On this occasion,

"Because you're only a new recruit and out of the kindness of my heart, and for no other reason,"

said Adjutant,

"I will not place you, 7287, whose number I will remember, on a charge or report you to Sergeant for other punitive action, but would remind you (naughty boy) that never, ever again will you fail to acknowledge the true position of all officers,"

who were clearly superior to myself.

It took some twelve months for this piece of pompous idiocy to be given an appropriate response, as a later chapter will show.

The most consistent occupation for we, the recruits, during this training period was marching. To be lined up in three ranks, equally distant from each other and made to walk in harmonious style, with arms moving to a certain height, eyes fixed rigidly ahead, clearly has a point. If the group need to get somewhere at the same time, it has great usefulness, especially in the first few days when the camp and its facilities were largely unknown, so that we all could arrive together, with no one getting lost or having forgotten the time! But the pointlessness of spending hour after hour being put through the paces of marching, turning, wheeling, saluting in unison, turning eyes to right or left on command, and dealing with a rifle, which many in the artillery would not have in their possession again throughout the rest of their service, was apparent to all but the most stupid. There were, of course, those who thought that they could get away with being sloppy or out of step or to be unaware of their right or left – but such misdemeanours, on the part of a few individuals, only produced one response from Sergeant. The whole group did it again and again and again until he was satisfied that there were no rebellious or unconnected spirits left in the group.

Having said that, there was one individual among the whole group who entered on the same day, and who made it quite clear to his very close friends that he was determined to get out of this whole business. He was not alone, but few succeeded whatever method they chose. His method was never to march correctly. It all started, for all the normal ones among us, with the left foot going forward first, accompanied by the right arm, but he would move his foot and arm on the same side of his body and continue to be at odds with everyone else. Whatever they did to him, he failed ever to march correctly and eventually, after medical assessment, he was discharged. What effort it took him, none but he knew.

If, in some moment of apparent relaxation of normality, when recruits and teachers could talk and a question was raised as to the value of all this, the answer was always the same. Discipline. This was given some reality by the older sergeants, who had been involved in the war, by them describing some infantry action, in which, when a command, whatever it be, came ringing from the rear, everyone must obey instinctively, without thought and instantaneously, otherwise that person would surely be dead.

One of the things that never seemed to happen in all this basic training was to take those who were less able or capable of doing what was required and separating them from the group for additional remedial training. The only understanding on the part of these training practitioners was that conformity of the whole group was the key to gaining successful soldiers.

There were other aspects of these weeks of initial training. One of which was to make assessments of us, and so determine our usefulness to the army. This involved our indicating our personal preferences and the filling in of many forms of different types, but largely about our previous experiences and attainments. There were also psychological assessments, ones that were in common use at the time, conducted by specialist NCO's who gave us tests to be completed and who followed these up with interviews. Some of this involved basic educational attainments, though what remedial measures were able to be put in place was not known to us recruits. As someone who had thought hard about becoming a teacher, it was natural for me to attempt to join the Education Corps, though with trained teachers, who had just completed their College courses, doing their national service, it was a hopeless quest. Instead it was suggested to me that I should consider myself as officer material and attend a War Office Selection Board (WOSB). This had considerable effect on my future service and will be developed further in another chapter.

There was also a deal of classroom work, sometimes, but not often, undertaken by our own sergeants, who would give only general preliminary talks about tactics. More often the classroom work was in the hands of specialist NCO's who were generally much more civilised than our sergeants. We were also shown a rifle, how to strip it down into its constituent parts and put it together again, to read maps, and to understand the general nature of King's Regulations as far as they affected us. Although I was never, throughout my two years, provided with a rifle, it seemed to be an understanding of all those involved in training us that we would have one as a personal responsibility and so would need to know how these things worked, and what was our personal maintenance responsibility and how it was to be carried out.

The first six weeks of initial training and assessment were thus very demanding, to say the least, but achieved their aim of limiting any individual characteristics and to get us working together. It also bonded us together as 'us' against 'them'! That was brought home to me towards the end, as our Sergeant, a burly rugby player, returned from a match in a pitiable state with his head torn and bloodied. We saw him as he returned for a shower before going off to the medical centre to be bandaged up. It was the only time he wasn't the bullying, shouting, horrible human being he thought was appropriate for a 'Sergeant'. There wasn't a moment's pity or sympathy for him, the common expressions being,

"Serve him bloody right."

Others were quite clear that they would love to have had the opportunity to do similar things to him.

3. Syncopated Swimming

The other requirement of troops is that they are fit and able to sustain considerable physical activity. So getting and keeping fit was a regular concern. This required regular 'route marches' out of the camp, or cross country runs, as well as sessions with the Physical Training instructors (PTi's) usually in the gym. The latter provided one of the only pleasant, fun sessions of the whole initial training. As an interesting diversion from the basic gym exercises, which my set of recruits liked if not enjoyed, was that one of the PTi's, who was a Sadlers Wells trained ballet dancer, also doing his national service, would, as part of his session, get everyone started on performing some simple action such as hopping from one leg to another, then he added a second action, probably using an arm or arms, acting in concert with or opposition to the first action. He would go on adding one action after another, all to be repeated in sequence, until people could no longer continue to keep up with the sequence. He would only end when there was only one or two left still performing – but he was never beaten! The difference in this activity against all the others was that it was done in fun and he made it an enjoyable exercise for all, and one in which he gained the respect of us all. Less enjoyable were forced marches or runs that were graded in severity according to the stage of training. We were led from relatively short runs, in PT kit, of one or two miles to longer runs in full uniform and carrying kit bags on one's back. These were exhausting for all and there were usually some who could not complete the run or forced march, especially if this was at a faster speed or a longer distance than usual.

One other person, Lt G, also a National Serviceman, gained our respect and treated us as human beings. He was very fit, and was likely, at the end of such a run or march, after we were given a few minutes to catch our breath and wait for the whole group to be together again, to challenge us to a further run within the camp.

"How about racing down to the end of the square and back again."

He would challenge and most of us looked at him in disbelief, but a few of us would accept the challenge. He always was the first back, but I was always in the leading group. All those who could manage the challenge gained respect in the process, chiefly Lt G, who was clearly the fittest among us! Later I met him socially, at church, but he never shared with me any of his personal details of how he came to be so fit.

All recruits were given medical examinations, though we had all been examined and found to be fit for service prior to our being called up. Whether any recruits who had medical conditions were diagnosed and able to be treated was something that I was not aware of, for no one in my intake was given further medical help or discharged due to medical conditions.

The other aspect of our initial training was to prepare us for military service, such as the classroom work to strip down, maintain and re-assemble a rifle, and there was also opportunity to test our ability on a rifle range. This was something that I did not do well – for the simple reason that I seemed unable to close my left eye and leave the right one open in order to see along the sight. This clearly skewed my ability to sight correctly and, whilst there were those who spotted that I was holding my head incorrectly in order to see out of my left eye, no attempt either to teach or train me or to provide me with a differently designed rifle ever took place. The 'old soldiers' responsible for our weapons training seemed simply to shrug their shoulders at my inability. I even overheard the comment that,

"If he ever gets into a tricky situation, he'll fire it alright!"

Fortunately, I was never placed in the position that I needed to fire a rifle, or anything else, to defend myself or others.

4. Can You Really Swim Well?

The ending of the six-week initial training course was a tense time for us all. Some were over the moon at their selection as mechanics, drivers, electricians or other 'trades', for they would receive first class training that would qualify them for a job, or, if already qualified, would provide them with further qualifications or opportunities for promotion. Some were even 'selected' to leave the Royal Artillery and join the Pioneer Corps, where the main, for some only, duties would involve manual labour. It was a reflective comment on society at large, for more time and energy was expended selecting those who were thought to be officers or had already obtained special skills as musicians, doctors or teachers, or indeed anyone suitable for specialist work. It felt to us that the sergeant's view was all that was required to be labelled a *'pick and shovel man'* and sent off to the Pioneer Corps. There were some among us who found reading or writing difficult but not impossible, but, as far as we were aware, no help or special provision was made available to them. Let's hope such help was given after they moved from initial training.

Because I was 'selected' as potential officer material and had been put down to attend a WOSB, I remained at Oswestry when the cohort I had arrived with finished their six weeks and moved on to an allocated regiment or training facility. Most, if not all, of those selected for officer assessment potential at WOSB seemed to have already left. It was not clear what would happen to me, with whom I would be based or to whom I was responsible. Somehow or another I was allocated to work with a sergeant dealing with the next batch of recruits and, in order to do so, was given a stripe to wear as an Acting Lance Bombardier (unpaid and unrecognised except by the new recruits). As far as it went, it was fun and I managed to be employed usefully in a number of ways. I even attended, in my Lance Bombardierial capacity, a week's practical training course of actual firing of guns at a firing range in the Brecon Beacons near Sennybridge. It was one of the coldest, bleakest and most pointless experiences of my life. We travelled in the back of three-tonne trucks in freezing January weather and found ourselves camping in a wild spot high in the hills, with no habitation nearby. The trainees protested, and their training staff had to deal with that, but it did not involve, neither did anything else, we support staff. We had nothing to do, except freeze! It was an uncomfortable and complete waste of my time. The trainees were, of course, kept busy and made to work, undertake runs and other physical activity that at least kept them warm.

Although the suggestion that I was suitable officer material had come out of the assessment process all recruits had undergone, no one had any responsibility to discuss the matter with me. I had reservations both as to my suitability, for the only situation in which I had control over or responsibility for others, was two years in the Boys Brigade. When I completed my school certificate, we moved as a family because of Dad's ministry, and this was the first time that I had opportunity to join any youth organisation. Our new church had a large congregation and I enthusiastically threw myself into all the activities I could, bearing in mind my sixth form studies. I must have presented a problem for the Boys Brigade officers, for few join such organisations when they are 16! I set about gaining badges, qualifications that one had achieved an acceptable grade in, say, understanding and tying knots or recognising species of trees and so on. So, in a short time, I was promoted to be a Staff Sergeant which was a training ground for potential officers. We did some marching at every session, so that we could take part in civic and other parades, but that was the only activity in which I held any responsibility.

I didn't think this qualified me to be an army officer and I had little concept of what it would mean in the forces' context, and I had further reservations about the lifestyle and financial implications. I had gathered that the officers dressed up in their posh uniforms some, if not most, evenings and attended their mess for dinner. These were very formal occasions, I gathered, in which correct behaviour was very important, though that behaviour could be very rumbustious on some occasions. The notion that I should spend my evenings dressed in formal rig out and expected to behave in ways to which I was not accustomed did not appeal to me at all. I had no idea what the pay for an officer would be and the uniform, even if one was provided with the basic one, would be expensive. Nor had I ever had the opportunity or desire to drink alcohol and considered myself to be teetotal, so I had no conception of what it would be to spend most evenings having a dinner with alcohol, in which the amount consumed seemed to be important and measured one's acceptability. I wasn't keen on, or looking forward to, the WOSB experience and had even less idea of what it would involve.

The actuality was little different. I was the only one from my intake at my particular selection so travelled with no one and knew no one present. Most of the others there were from a different background to myself; many from public schools, who, to some extent, knew each other. Some ordinarily spoke in authoritarian language and manner. They expected to be selected and to rule. It seemed as if they were born to it – unlike me! There were, of course, written tests to undertake and interviews with individual selectors – none of us had any idea how we progressed in these. There were group discussions and I doubt if I did well in those as the confident, articulate and opinionated dominated. I probably said little, just observed. I don't think it was much better in the group activities, about which many were well informed, unlike me. For these we were broken into small groups of five or six and set some task in which improvisation and initiative were to be shown. Again, some seemed to know exactly what was expected and even to have been informed of the 'tricks of the trade', as it were, by friends who had already been through the experience. Again, it was not a metier in which I would naturally shine.

It was thus of little surprise to me that I was not selected for officer training and I returned to Oswestry to resume my one-temporary-stripe behaviour without any idea as to what was to happen next. It took a few weeks – and I was happy enough – until I was informed that I would become a Technical Assistant, and there were even a few classes to initiate me into what that actually meant. Perhaps, of greater significance was that I could go home every weekend and, as home was only two stations down the line, it was affordable.

I had started at the beginning of September, it was now January, and after five months based at the Oswestry camp I was suddenly returned to being an ordinary recruit at the end of initial training and was dispatched, with many others, to join the 18th Royal Artillery Regiment in Lancaster. As an attendee at WOSB, it was my luck that the War Office had responsibility for my future situation. January was the time their posting arrived.

5. Starting to Get Somewhere

As soon as we had arrived, late on a Thursday, in Lancaster barracks, it was made clear to us that many of us would be moving on immediately. Information was minimal but Lancaster camp couldn't contain all the regiment, so a large part of the regiment was based at Preston Barracks. New arrivals were being, it seemed to us, arbitrarily placed in one or other camp. It was a temporary arrangement because we would all be going to Salisbury Plain shortly!

So, Saturday morning saw a number of us travelling to Preston, 20 miles south on the main A6 road. I happened to be sitting in the cab with the driver and, as we approached Fulwood, in Preston, we stopped at traffic lights, and to the left, on the corner, was a large Methodist Church, so I said to the driver,

"Are the barracks much further?"

He replied,

"No, we turn left here and it's just a few minutes up the road to the barracks."

I made a mental note that, assuming that the guard duty roster had already been prepared, I would be free on the following morning, Sunday, and would be able to attend this church. It took only a glance at the church notice board as we passed to discover the time of the morning service and firm up my plan.

Entrance to Fulwood Barracks

Living Quarters, Fulwood Barracks, Preston

That is, in fact, what happened, and so began one of the most pleasant interludes and experiences of my life. As I had with me only my army uniform, I stood out in the congregation being somewhat visible among everyone else in their usual clothes and, after the morning worship concluded, many of the congregation came, welcomed me and said how pleased they were to see me. Among them was a tall attractive lady who, having ascertained that I was stationed at the Fulwood barracks, explained that they did not normally see soldiers from the barracks in their congregation because the chaplain at the barracks was based at a different church in another direction. She went on to explain that her husband was not at church that morning but she would like me to walk home with her, as it was almost on the way back to the barracks, to meet him. Gathering her young son, John, aged about six or seven, that is what we did. When we arrived at their large detached home, I found Mr Smith to be rather older than his wife, and shorter, but bubbly and full of fun and mischief. I was immediately made to feel at home and invited to return for tea. Thus I discovered, was welcomed into, and became a temporary member of the Smith family.

It turned out that we were destined to be in Preston for only a few weeks but in that time the Smith's family home became my second home. It didn't take long to discover that Mr Smith and his brothers ran one of the largest businesses in the area, with three cotton mills and some specialisation in making velvet cloth of the highest quality. Clearly their financial situation was very different from mine, but that mattered not. I was invited to go out with them on Saturdays into Lytham St Annes, Blackpool or the surrounding beautiful Lancashire countryside. I was able to have luxurious baths and for the first time ever met a wall heater in the bathroom. Such luxury I had never met before in any of our Methodist Church manses! Once I was somehow able to get an afternoon off and Mr Smith took me round one of the mills, showing and explaining the processes. As with most Lancashire mills, the noise all the looms made meant that it was impossible for us to talk, but it was very apparent that he was liked and respected by the workers, knowing both them, their work and often their families very well. It made sense when he explained that he visited them if and when sickness or other trouble came to them. He talked to me and we discussed matters in a way that good fathers would do with their teenage sons.

I will never forget an evening when he and I sat talking, and after some time he casually said,

"If you suddenly came by, say, £5 what would you do with it?"

After replying that such an eventuality was very unlikely that I couldn't really imagine it, he playfully, but persistently, pursued the matter. I found it hard to conceive such an event. Eventually, as I was studying at the time to become a lay preacher in the church, I said to him that I thought I would use it to buy books.

"Good," he said as he pulled out his wallet and took out a £5 note, "I think I expected you to say something like that, so enjoy your books," as he handed me the note.

Nothing like that had ever happened to me before, and I cannot forget the kindness and generosity of both Mr and Mrs Smith, and be grateful for the links that were made with my family and the ongoing contact that they and my parents enjoyed for many years. My final meeting took place many years later, and after Mr Smith had died, when I was invited to preach at a special service in one of the Preston Methodist churches, and there in the congregation were Mrs Smith and John, so typical, unassuming and such a pleasure to meet such a wonderful family.

There was a similar sense of purpose and opportunity back in the barracks. As a Technical Assistant, I began to undertake training sessions to both understand the work they did and be equipped to undertake it efficiently. It was work that I enjoyed and built on my school geography and my interest in maps. In those days, long before the internet, with its modern aids, Technical Assistants had the responsibility accurately to locate, on maps, the position of the guns and the target, and from those positions to calculate and inform the gunners of the direction and distance needed for the gun's shells to hit the target. Assuming the shells were observed as they landed, we then received observations that the shell had landed so far right or left, fell short or had gone past the target by so many yards, and we then translated that into further amended instructions. If it was only a short distance, the officer in the command post would translate the distance into something like,

"One degree left. Fire!"

to the gunners. If the distances were greater, we would need to do further calculations so that accurate directions could be given to the gunners.

The purpose of our gathering at both Lancaster and Fulwood Barracks, we discovered, was that we were to move, as soon as we were fully operational, to Larkhill Barracks on Salisbury Plain to be the regiment attached to the School of Artillery. This meant that the regiment's establishment was increasing to that of wartime, rather than the existing peacetime, numbers and posts, and that meant that further troops were regularly arriving. But more of that later.

It was a pleasant time at Fulwood Barracks. Some of my colleagues had played hockey at school and when we found some nets and sticks we managed to play a few games together. As I had only ever played football, this was a new, challenging, but enormously pleasant experience. As a short distance runner, I was very quick and sharp moving around, but much less proficient in handling the hockey stick to keep it and the ball low. Had they been 'proper' games, I would have been severely disciplined!

The time there was also my introduction to guard duty, a serious but boring chore that consumed evenings that might otherwise have been our leisure time. The procedure was that Daily Orders would be posted on the noticeboard and, amongst other matters, those who were to do guard duty – those responsible for guarding the site – after working hours would be announced. For those named, it meant being excused normal duty, for an hour, in order to get ready and parade at 1630 hrs or thereabouts. It was normal, both there and later, in this Regiment that six people were required as the guard, who would then work in pairs, taking it in turn to guard the perimeter fence and camp, generally for two hours and then have four hours to 'rest'. In the 12 hours from 1800 hrs to 0600 hrs, each would have four hours walking round and eight to rest. Daily Orders would name eight people and these had to appear, dressed in their best uniform (we had two issued, a best and a working one) and with everything in spick and span condition, with boots, buttons and badges all polished and shining. The duty Sergeant, as Guard Commander, would instruct us in the duties that we would have to perform throughout the evening and check that everything was in order, and each man was prepared and ready for the inspection of the Duty Officer. Woe betide anyone failing to meet the high standards expected, for he would be told off and might even be punished. That over, the Duty Officer would inspect us all again. Some were very ready to offer reprimands and other punishments to anyone who was not turned out to his satisfaction. The Duty Officer then selected two people out of the guard. One person was the worst turned out in the Duty Officer's view and would have to go and change and skivvy for the guard for the rest of the night. This would involve cleaning the Guardroom, collecting and returning the guard's evening meal and breakfast, running errands, and doing any chores that were required or that the sergeant could invent. The other nominee was the 'stick man', the one in the Duty Officer's view who was the best turned out. He was effectively excused all further duties, nor be required to attend, far less stay, in the guardroom, though he would normally be expected to remain in the camp and some Guard Commanders would allocate some minor duties. If the sergeant had a particular grudge against the chosen man, then he might even make some requirements.

All this 'guard duty' became pleasant for me because I was consistently chosen as Stick Man and never did guard duty at Preston. The reason for this was relatively simple in that most soldiers went out in the evenings to the pub or attempting to pull women, and so dressed in their best uniforms. Whenever I went out, I never went to pubs, as did others, or got into scrapes or fights. So, whilst their best uniforms inevitably became used, scruffy or dirty and looked as worn and as used as they, in fact, were, my best uniform was almost like new, as were my 'brown' boots! On my visits to the Smith family or on outings with them, I wore my ordinary civilian clothes, for we were allowed civilian clothes. A pattern became established whereby, almost every day, someone would approach me to ask if they could borrow my uniform and/or boots for the guard parade. I always agreed on condition that the items were returned to me on my terms. These were that, once the parade was over, they changed out of my uniform, which would be returned to me the next day in the same condition that I had lent it out, having been pressed. The same applied to boots, which would have to be cleaned and polished so that they were returned to me in the same condition as they left. My uniform seemed, day after day, to get the 'stick man' nomination and so I had a uniform that got worn for 15–20 minutes that day and then pressed and returned to me in pristine condition! No one ever failed to keep the condition, my uniform gracing the body of so many chosen 'stick men', who were simply glad to have avoided the unpleasant guard duty. For me, it meant my uniform was well looked after! The whole arrangement was beneficial to all, especially me, and eventually, as I recall later, through my uniform I achieved my one and only moment of passing glory!

After a few weeks at Fulwood Barracks, we moved to Larkhill Camp on Salisbury plain close to the national School of Artillery. It was their job to train officers and also Warrant Officers as Inspector Gunners. These were the technical experts and advisers on the guns used by the artillery and were those who were expected to train others, monitor standards, resolve technical problems and ensure that the highest standards were maintained. They were supreme and could not be overruled by anyone, whatever his rank, in regard to technical matters, for example whether a damaged gun was fit to fire. The School was also attended by very senior officers going through refresher and training courses where tactical matters were discussed and taught. The School always had a regiment, at full wartime establishment, based nearby, and whose troops, guns, and equipment could be used when the 'students' at the School undertook exercises. Apart from any regiment actively involved in a war zone, this was the premier task of any regiment in the RA.

Lark Hill Camp, Salisbury Plain

School of Artillery, Lark Hill Salisbury Plain

The CO made it very clear that his regiment would only be able to replace the 5th RHA Regiment, at the School, when we were judged by him and the senior staff at the School to be fit for purpose. So, we were all undertaking daily training exercises to bring ourselves to the standard required and there grew up some friendly competition between the respective Troops. Each Troop consisted of four guns, with their necessary ammunition, transport and gunners, a command post with Troop Commander, Junior Officers, Technical Assistant, Wireless Operators, as well as Cooks and other support staff. I was the 'Tech Ack' in B Troop and discovered quickly that it carried some responsibilities and rewards. As a troop, those below the rank of sergeant lived in a standard Nissen Hut, which provided one small room in addition to the main room where everyone slept. Our Sergeant Major ordered me, as TA, to be responsible at all times for the technical equipment used by the Troop. This technical equipment lived in the small room and that also became my bedroom. In one sense, it wasn't a great deal – maps, board, compasses, binoculars, tripods and theodolites are not the most decorative things to have in a bedroom! The responsibility that came with the job was, as our Sergeant Major commanded me,

"If anything goes missing or gets damaged, be it on your head, lad."

So I had a room to myself, though I slept with all this stuff arranged around the room. The room had a lock on the door as well! Understandably I welcomed the privacy.

This simple fact made a massive difference to my life for, long before the Troops were accounted, by the CO, capable of working with the School, the School would require a Command Post and its equipment for some of their exercises. Our Sergeant Major's decision was that B Troop's equipment or Command Post was not to be used without my presence, for the equipment was my responsibility. In fact, in practice, I was the senior person from our regiment present on such occasions – even though I had nothing to do other than ensure that all the equipment was returned from course members and was in good working order. B Troop's Command Post and Tech Ack, were the first in the regiment to be judged able to be used by the School. What wonderful days I had as we roamed, from one firing range to another, across the glorious countryside of the Plain, with a 15cwt truck and some equipment which simply I had to oversee.

Earlier I said I would return to continue the story of the Training Camp Adjutant and his petty rebuke when I failed to see him and salute. Many of the courses at the School were attended by officers going through refresher training courses. One morning when I was out with the School and responsible for our Command Post and equipment, who should I see but Mr Adjutant, no longer the preening shouter at raw recruits, but an uncomfortable member of a course in which he was not shining. I did not have to acknowledge him nor any of the other 'students' but we recognised each other and as the morning progressed it became very clear to me that he was not coping. He couldn't understand some of the things he was being taught and was required to do. One of the cardinal rules of the School was that their students were required not to ask any of us from the regiment for help. They were to seek help from, or discuss their problems with, the course instructors who were available for that purpose. However, Mr Adjutant kept looking at me with eyes that begged for help. I'm not sorry that I kept him dangling throughout the morning, by carrying out my orders to the letter and refusing to assist when he mislaid a piece of equipment, even though I would be aware of its location! Eventually just once or twice I raised an eyebrow when he was making an error or pointed a finger in a way that would help him. I felt he got his comeuppance and knew it!

The spring and summer months of 1951 were a joy for me. Apart from anything else there was time to relax, meet some of the other lads with whom I did not normally meet, such as the drivers. It even gave me my very first chance to have a go at driving. Using a 15cwt truck in a large area of down land, I was first shown how to engage gear and steer. Sometimes it was only for a very short distance, but it gave me a taste. These contacts and experience enabled me, one evening after our meal, to make my way to the vehicle park or garage, an open fronted shed, on an occasion when the vehicles had returned late and in a very dirty condition. At such times, the responsible drivers were still clearing up, washing and checking on their vehicles, as they were on this day. I did not want to get in their way, for they did not get dinner until their work was finished! But they were friendly and I was allowed to sit in a truck and different drivers would show me the gears and how to let out the clutch and explained the principles. On one of the very early occasions, to the consternation of all those present, I let out the clutch with the Jeep engine running! Having engaged gear, it shot forward on to the road way, the other side of which was the office building. To the amazement and relief of all, I managed to turn onto the road and miss the building – and stop! The consequences if I had not managed this manoeuvre would have been very serious with a jeep damaged possibly seriously, maybe even me too, to say nothing of the impact on the office building – and all without any permission! Some of the things I learned or discovered were not part of the intention of the army or the politicians who designed National Service, but served me in good stead. Five years later, after only a few trips out with family members in the only car available to me, I took and passed my test first time and have had over 60 years of constant driving with only a couple of very minor incidents!

As well as such recreation, there was a job to be done and it too was a pleasure. Through all the machinations of initial training and WOSB, I had never been properly graded as a TA. I knew my job and was on top of it and was accepted and respected by all. Our Sergeant Major no longer screamed at me, as he did everyone else, but had proper conversations, knowing, I assume, that I was capable of handling the responsibilities he had given me without recourse to him. That side of his responsibilities could be forgotten by him, it was taken care of. The Troop CO, Captain H, was a great guy – a true commander of men, quietly spoken, for he didn't need to raise his voice, a master of his job and respected by all. Typical of him was one occasion in the early days, when we were still being tested and tried, and there seemed to have been some panic with people shouting commands, and changing them. In the rush and melee, I got confused and made a mistake, and a senior officer, acting as Observer, bellowed down the phone at me. Before I could even think what it was about, the CO was by my side with an arm round my shoulder and a quiet calming word in my ear,

"OK, let's just re-check that shall we? Then you'll be OK."

No one else knew, the problem was sorted, my respect for Captain Harris grew and the respect I had from others, including the Sergeant Major, was not diminished.

The lads in the Troop also seemed to value my non-alcoholic, Christian lifestyle, for as they said,

"Peter, what would we do without you on a Friday night when we get back pissed? We need you to help us into bed – and you always do, you're OK."

The Troop Commander, Captain H, had an even greater impact on me and my service, without his intention. One morning I was summoned to his office. He sat me down and told me that he thought I was not achieving my potential. He wanted to recommend me for a WOSB, arguing that I was officer material. As we talked, he wanted to know why I had not been selected at my previous WOSB visit and encouraged me to think of that not as a failure but a learning experience. I was reluctant to agree and when pressed said that I did not think I could afford to be an officer, though I still had no idea if and why that would be the case. After some discussion he replied,

"You know we all have to cut our coat according to our cloth."

To which I remember I replied,

"Yes, but you have to have some cloth to cut, sir!"

He smiled and eventually I agreed for him to recommend me if he felt that was right and he so wanted. He did, and it was a similar experience for me as on the previous visit. In fact, I think I was even more disenchanted with it and really didn't want to be selected. I wasn't.

That WOSB visit had greater repercussions than either Capt. H or I imagined in that, for the second time, it was now the responsibility of the War Office to place me in the most advantageous place for the army! They failed to notice that they had already, on my previous attendance at a WOSB, sent me to the 18th Regiment as part of that programme – but decided that I should now go to join the United Nations Divisional Force in Korea.

6. Floating

Although the initial spelling out to we raw recruits made it clear to us that we belonged body and soul to His Majesty's army lords and masters, there clearly was some time and opportunity to relax and have some freedom to do and be as we pleased.

Once the initial training weeks were complete, opportunity arose at Oswestry, mostly at weekends, when it was possible for me to return home. But I was also in the process of studying and working for my Methodist Local Preachers' examinations and was continuing to preach on some Sundays. I was able to take my bicycle to the camp and this enabled me to cycle into Oswestry town on some evenings, though there wasn't much activity taking place there that interested me. The cycle also allowed me to cycle into some of the border Welsh villages to conduct church services. They were usually located well up in the hills, which seemed like mountains when cycling! As the autumn passed into winter, services were held in the afternoon to avoid people travelling in the night time darkness. So, I had chance to see some of the beautiful Border countryside. Most services were uneventful, but I still remember one with some wonderment at my youthful brashness. There were few in the congregation so the singing was somewhat desultory at best. Well into the service I had chosen a hymn without any alternative tune to the one set in the Methodist Hymn Book. The organist lady was playing a harmonium, located to the left below the pulpit, and she faced me. As the first verse came to a close, she looked at me and said,

"I'm sorry but we don't know this."

This had been apparent to me from the first bars and I had been frantically thinking what else I could do. There was no alternative tune and I couldn't immediately think of a different hymn for us to sing, so, in response, having looked at the blank faces of the small congregation in front of me, I replied,

"Well, I do, so perhaps we'll carry on singing it and folk can join in when they can!"

It was virtually a solo and I have remained chastened at what I put the poor lady organist through, for she didn't know the music well at all.

There were also some young people's activities in the church at Oswestry to which I was welcomed and was able to attend when I wasn't at home at the weekends.

The few weeks spent in Preston was, of course, a fantastic opportunity to share in the activities of the Smith family. My, was I fortunate, to find a family like that even though it seemed a relatively normal thing to happen to a young Christian lad lost.

There was more opportunity on Salisbury Plain to share in the worship and activities of the Methodist church at Amesbury where the congregation were well used to soldiers, from a number of the locally based camps, attending their services. I was still preaching as opportunity presented itself, but my most regular activity was the Saturday visit to Salisbury. As a historic town, there were plenty of things to see and do on an afternoon and, as I cycled or walked, I could go via Sarum, though the historic site was little more than a mound then, or visit the Cathedral or other historic places. Saturday evenings were taken up with the Repertory Theatre with its weekly cycle of plays. I enjoyed them immensely.

Looking back, I am impressed at how much I must have travelled. Walking into Salisbury, some 11 or 12 miles, was common, though I would catch a bus back to Amesbury at night. However, some of the walking was more problematic.

With all the camps on the Plain, there would be many soldiers each weekend able to go home, or some other place, starting late on Friday afternoons, and coaches were provided from the camps to Andover railway station. The return journey would be taken on Sunday night on a train leaving from Paddington station in London at midnight, back to Andover, where coaches would return we squaddies to our respective camps. I used this transport system a couple of times without incident. I then had to return home, to Shropshire, for an oral examination in connection with my Local Preacher training. So, I had negotiated a pass allowing me to return on Monday night, ready for inspection at 06:30 on Tuesday morning. I arrived safely and in good time at Paddington only to find that the midnight train to Andover ran only on Sunday nights. It was a special service for we service folk! I had no other option but to catch the mail train, which shed its postal deliveries at every station on the line but did not call or stop at Andover! It got me to Salisbury three or four hours later. Naturally it was also the one occasion when I had a trunk full of things I was taking back to camp from home, as I had got my own room by then. How was I to get myself and a trunk from Salisbury station to Larkhill Camp? The only option was, somehow, to leave the trunk at the station. There was no one about at all, and the Left Luggage office was securely closed. There was no ability to leave my trunk at the station. I went out to the street and a few doors down was the police station, so I went in. The Desk Sergeant greeted me,

"And what can I do for you, lad?"

"Well, sir, I've just got off the mail train and I've got to walk to Lark Hill Camp by six o'clock, so can I leave my trunk here for safe keeping until I can collect it later today?"

"No, lad, that won't be possible. This isn't a Left Luggage office, you know."

"Yes, I do know that, Sergeant, but this is an emergency for me. Surely, you could just keep my trunk behind the counter here for a few hours?"

"No, lad, I couldn't."

"You wouldn't have any other suggestions, would you, Sergeant? No other place where it could stay?"

"No. I've told you we're not a left luggage office at all. The only thing we can take in is Lost Property."

"Well, couldn't you say you'd found it and taken it in for safe keeping and I can claim it later?"

"You're a persistent bugger, aren't you? Why don't you just get off and leave me to my work?"

"It's just what I do with this trunk, that's the problem, Sergeant."

"Well, I'm not allowing you to leave it here. It's not allowed."

"OK! So, I think the only thing I can do is go outside and leave my trunk there. Then you'll find it and have to bring it in as lost property, won't you."

"I'm not so sure about that, either. I might not have to go outside and find it. You'd be a lot safer taking it with you. And that's my final advice to you, laddy. Go on, I've got work to do."

I had no option but to assume that he would take the blooming trunk in. I hoped that I had somehow melted his heart and so with no more ado I took myself and the trunk outside. On the pavement, I removed the few valuables and left the trunk where it was bound to be seen. I hoped that, if the sergeant wasn't going to help, some early morning workman would carry it in and say that he had found it lying on the pavement in front of the police station. With that I had to set off and make good speed to complete the 12 or so miles in time to be on parade, only troubled that I didn't know what the day's programme was and whether I was supposed to be parading with all our kit to go off with a School of Artillery party! In that case, I would have to have some good reasons sorted out as to why I wasn't ready. In fact, it wasn't a problem, for we had no such action that day.

Whatever actually happened to my trunk I don't know, for I returned once the day's work was done, simply asking if someone had handed in a trunk, for I had had to leave mine during the night. It was there and returned to me, without a word. So, I suspect the sergeant, for all his officious official act, had actually taken the trunk into his safekeeping. At least I have always thought that is what must have happened – for he really was a kind man!

7. A Reflective Interlude

A couple of days after I was informed that I was to be posted to Korea, the chief clerk in the Regimental office sought me out and took me aside for a chat. This was somewhat unusual for I had had little to do with him. He began by being very circumspect and saying that he had been considering whether he should maintain confidentiality or speak to me.

But I think you have a right to know exactly what happened. When Captain H set off from the office, it was to see you to tell you something that you must still keep confidential. The CO has been arguing with the School of Artillery and the War Office that he can't be expected to produce this regiment with the skills he thinks the School needs without he has at least two Inspector Gunners [IG's] on the regiment's staff. The School says there aren't any to be allocated but he has persuaded them that he can provide two men from the regiment who are capable of being trained as Warrant Officer IG's. They will be the first National Servicemen to have achieved that position, indeed National Servicemen have not normally attended the School. Captain H was on his way to tell you this and that you were to join the School next month, in September, as one of the two. I had to run after him and bring him back because a signal had just been received from the War Office with your posting to Korea. There's nothing that we can do about that, and the thing with the School is now being re-considered. It doesn't make any difference to you – but I think you ought to know what the situation was.

There wasn't much that I could say and nothing I, or anyone else, could do, other than to thank him for his information, which I valued. This was particularly so as my mind was pre-occupied by the implications of a posting to Korea. It was a conflict that we all knew something, if very little, about. Whilst the wider geo-political factors might be blurred in our minds, the one thing we all knew was that the conflict had caused many deaths among British troops. For people such as me, with no experience of warfare at all, nor any real understanding of where Korea was and what it was like there, sorting out my feelings was not an easy task. As far as I was concerned, it seemed a difficult place to be, in that it was in Asia, the other side of the world, in a place where things were very different from Europe. What messages came to us in radio news bulletins, that I was aware of, seemed to indicate that the nature of the fighting was different from what had occurred in the war in Europe.

As I considered the matter, it seemed to me a dangerous place to be and in the days that followed I came to a firm conviction that I would not return from it.

I feel certain I will die.

There was, of course, a countervailing voice inside me holding out some doubt about that, especially for me as a committed Christian.

For I am already clear that I feel a calling, a calling from God to the ordained, to the ordained ministry of the church – and thus, I could, as many others in the same position probably did, assume that God will protect me. After all, if God has a purpose for me, surely that will be fulfilled in His own way?

Two voices speaking inside and I could, in no sense, be certain as to which was right. But, on balance, it was the first that seemed the more likely. I didn't feel in any way so special that everything would somehow be turned around so that I would not go. The mighty army seemed a vast and powerful machine that would have its way come what may, and, if there was anything special in me, it had already been rejected by some impersonal machinery called the 'war office'. With no idea at all about the nature of the actual fighting in this different war, there was nothing in my mind to alter a simple equation; fighting in any war means death for most soldiers. I settled for that!

Having arrived at that speculative conclusion, it was something I could not share with anyone. The lads around me, with the best of intentions, would have scoffed and jockeyed me out of such morbid thoughts. There was clearly to be no way that I could share my thoughts with my parents or girlfriend. What good could it do them? It would only worry and disturb them and it was so much better that I keep silent about it. And I did. I was on my own, alone, with only my own thoughts.

So, in myself, I faced the prospect of death and what it would mean for me. As I look back on the experience, remembered as if it were yesterday, I see it as a process that is today recognised as one common stage in a grief process. That begins with a sense of denial and of isolation. It continues with a sense of anger;

Why have I been selected? After all I am only a National Serviceman, and it was no part of my or of general thinking that, as such, I should serve in a theatre of war and possibly be killed. When I added to that the message I had just received, to the effect that there was a special role that I had been chosen, by those who knew me, to fulfil, after training in the School of Artillery – a role that few could be expected to undertake – it seemed a very ill considered thing to send me, obviously by some mechanistic system that just moved numbers about.

Thus, my thoughts went. I don't think I became depressed, but matters lay heavy on my heart. Life would be cut short, but then I had few expectations of life. Even my future occupation was in no way certain. But I already had a firm sense that God was calling me to the ministry of the church. That had not been an easy road to travel, for I had started from the position that I had no desire to work as my father worked. All those who had, through the years, patted me on the shoulder and said,

"And are you going to be a minister like your father?" had received a very blunt negative reply.

But things had changed, for the idea had recently taken root and I had begun training as a lay preacher but, for me in my ignorance, that had seemed to be the easy part of ministry. That was the element I felt I could fulfil. What had filled me with dread was the thought of helping folk whose child had been killed, or sitting for a couple of hours every week reading and talking with a seriously disabled woman or elderly man – things I knew my father had done. And there were many other aspects that I could not imagine undertaking. Those issues and thoughts had troubled me for long until, months ago, I had spent an evening with a friend, who was very disturbed and upset about something so that we talked of nothing else, yet she had seemed so much better and calmer when I left. As I walked home that night, I heard a clear voice saying, in answer to all my doubts,

"And who says you couldn't do such things?"

That was the turning point that led me to explore further seeking to candidate for the ministry. So, after all, I had a purpose, an idea of what I wanted to be and do. These matters were heavy on my heart and mind.

As a Christian I had, of course, certain fundamental certainties that this life was not the end of everything and that death was but an entrance into a different existence that was completely directed by God. At 19, I wasn't very sophisticated, and my thoughts and ideas were limited but, by the end of the process through which I went, I became certain that there was nothing ultimately to fear. I no more wanted to die than anyone else, but, if that was to happen, it would be within God's oversight. I had arrived at an uneasy acceptance of what could not be changed.

I went home for my two weeks' embarkation leave calm and relatively unperturbed, and told no one of the spiritual journey I had just travelled within myself. In later years, I have been thankful for that journey as I ministered to the dying and the bereaved. It was a journey that I had taken, however imperfectly, and without which I would have had little true understanding of what grief and loss meant for so many.

My dad didn't accept matters lying down, for he spoke with folk in the church and, unknown to me then, but revealed a short time later, the church did raise my situation with the army authorities who, nevertheless, maintained that the original decision was to be kept.

8. *Momentary Passing Glory*

At the end of the embarkation leave, I reported to Woolwich Arsenal Barracks in South East London, that was then the major headquarters of the Royal Artillery. This was something of a terrifying experience in that the barracks were bigger than any other camp I had been in and whenever we paraded there seemed to be thousands of us. As we had all come from different locations, very few of us knew anyone else and the situations we were in were different – we going abroad, others returning from abroad, and 'abroad' meant so many different things. I certainly felt very uncertain about my situation and it was inevitably a lonely time. It was also a busy time of being processed, with medical examinations, injections to vaccinate us from diseases, most of which most of us had never even heard about. Every single injection was followed by a period of marching, swinging our arms higher than was normal,

"In order to get the circulation really flowing,"

we were told, and so help the inoculation to be effective!

We also had to obtain a new set of clothing. We had to hand in the second 'ordinary' or everyday uniform and keep our best one. After doing that we were paraded, kitted out in our best khaki outfit. It was the longest and most boring parade we had to endure, seeming to go on for hours. First one inspection, then another by NCO's, and then more by officers, increasing in seniority, who came and sometimes made comments of disapproval at the state of a man's uniform. It then became clear to us that not every section of the parade was being 'inspected' in this way by the different inspection groups. In the section where I was, there seemed to be more of these sets of inspecting people than in other parts of the parade, and they came past and nodded and carried on. Eventually after a long time of waiting, when nothing at all happened and we were all thoroughly fed up and bored, another group of officers appeared and a murmur went around,

"It's the Adjutant General himself."

This group proceeded, as had most of the other groups, not looking at every section but at one or two, and then they appeared at the section I was in. This silent group of red braided men, betokening at least that they were Brigadiers, slowly processed until at last they stood in front of me, especially this older man, with red lapels and gold bits all over his uniform, who came forward and looked me up and down. Whatever was this? What did it mean? Was I in some sort of trouble? Finally, he spoke,

"Is this a new uniform you have recently been given?" he asked.

"No, sir."

And some other red-braided officer spoke quietly to him words that I was unable to catch.

"So how long have you been in the Army?"

"A year, since last September, sir."

And then a conversation followed between the great man and the one on his left to the extent that they said it was remarkable, and then the junior of the two said,

"It's as you have always said, sir, it is possible for these uniforms to be kept in this A1 condition. This man proves it, we don't need to make any alternative arrangement."

With a final turning to me the Adjutant General said,

"Well done, you are an example to everyone, showing how well a uniform can be kept."

With that they moved on and away from the parade.

Thanks to all the Stick Men who have looked after my uniform!

I thought – and finally, we could be dismissed.

To explain what lay behind this, I remind of the practice at Preston Barracks, which was general in all my postings, that two more than the required number for the guard being named and the best kitted being chosen as Stick Man, who did no guard duties as such.

9. Indecision – Going or Staying?

At the end of my embarkation leave, I reported to Woolwich Arsenal for a few very busy days, supposedly preparing us to leave the country. The preparation consisted in changing our uniform, medical examinations and vaccinations but little in the way of information. There was a gradual understanding that we would be going to Southampton to board a ship there. We even got to know, from where I cannot now imagine, that it was called HMS Devonshire. If Woolwich seemed busy, it was organised and routinised, and we moved from one stage to another and another with the feeling that those in control knew what they were about, if we didn't. It was a well-oiled machine!

It was another matter when we arrived on the holding area of the dockside. We were stood around, brought together, stood at ease again. There were knots of officers talking animatedly not far away – though about what nobody knew. Finally, we were brought to stand in the normal three ranks and an announcement was made.

"Has anyone here requested not to sail, on compassionate or other similar grounds?"

Seeing that there were some, including me, we were ordered to step forward and were taken to one side. We were each then questioned as to the circumstances of our appeal not to sail. A few were rejected and sent back to join the others. I was not among them when I explained that I was a candidate for the ministry of the Methodist Church, and the normal procedure was that all candidates would be required to sit some examinations and to go through a series of local and district committees and groups, culminating in a three-day national selection procedure next June. I understood the Church had asked for me not to be sent abroad as this would negate the normal selection procedure.

A group of about 30 of us were set aside. More discussions and consultations between officers took place, but it was clear to us, as we stood waiting, that men in another building were boarding the ship in an obviously ordered manner. We gathered that these were the Royal Norfolk Regiment who would form the bulk of the passengers. Of the remainder, there were groups of engineers, Military Police, other specialists and Medical and Service Corps personnel, in addition to the largest of such smaller contingents, we from the Royal Artillery. As the day progressed and we continued to stand around waiting, the group of 30 got reduced, then returned to the original number and then slowly reduced by one or two here or there who were returned to their original groups. Finally, we were down to 12 and then eight. I was still among them, but we had no idea what was happening and whether we were going or not. Was there room on this boat or not? Who and why would people be selected to travel or to stay? No one seemed accurately to know. However, at long last, we were marched up the gang plank because someone had discovered that there were just eight spare places in someone else's quarters.

It didn't take us long to discover that we were placed in a sergeants' billet. They were not too pleased to discover that we were to be thrust among them, though they were pleasant enough and helped us settle in. Within a couple of days, they complained that it was inappropriate to have ordinary rank soldiers like ourselves billeted with them and somewhere else should be found for us. Some shuffling took place, and some eight Military Police were discovered who could be accommodated more appropriately with the sergeants. We were accommodated in the place the Military Police personnel had vacated. It was still a separate area, which proved to be quite a pleasant and small area close to that of the families who were also travelling to join their husbands or fathers in Aden, Colombo, Singapore or Hong Kong. It was quite unlike the general conditions for the majority of those on board, who were accommodated below decks in what, I later found out, were generally thought to be the worst conditions of any of the regular troopships.

10. Sailing – Discovering the World

View of Port Said showing the illuminated advertising signs

Once on the boat, because of our location and separation from our original units, we were able to participate in a number of things others could only dream about. Two of us obtained secure employment for the whole journey looking after the few children on board and 'teaching' them. This was a very different and enjoyable experience compared to the Royal Norfolk men, who continued to train daily on the decks, deployed in attacking or defending positions about the ship's housing and equipment and firing many rounds into targets on the sea. Because we were located on the deck with the families, we were aware of concerts and similar activities that were being held most evenings, and two of us had the timidity to join one such concert. It was a revelation to me, who had twice not wanted to be considered as officer material, to find myself mixing with officers and their families who were all welcoming and respectful. We engaged in normal conversations and were treated as normally as they treated each other. Such normality and respect was so unusual a part of my previous experience of the army, that I felt a normal human being once more.

For someone who had never travelled outside the UK before, the journey was an amazing experience. The Bay of Biscay lived up to its reputation and I, like many others, found we had very unsettled stomachs! But then to sail within sight of the Iberian Peninsula was breath-taking, as was rounding Gibraltar. Then our arrival at our first stop in Port Said, Egypt, was an eye opener. We arrived during the night and I walked out on deck the next morning to be greeted by massive neon advertising signs that were such a surprise, especially as they were for the very things that we would consume at home, such as Bovril, Cadbury's Chocolate, etc. All my life I had been brought up on the idea that Africa and all such other places were peopled by backward natives for whom modern civilisation had not yet arrived! We were allowed ashore, but it was very difficult for those of us who couldn't afford taxis and were walking to get beyond the docks, for the constant pestering by tricksters and to a lesser degree beggars. It was also my first experience of local boats mooring alongside and sellers prepared to hoist up fruit and any trinkets they had for sale to passengers on deck. Nor were the children left out of the possible bonanza from a passenger boat in dock. They swam around, held on to the restraining ropes and, whenever they could persuade someone to throw a coin, would dive to retrieve it. They were experts indeed, with skills far beyond most of us. As a supposedly educated young Englishman, but very naive, I began to have my eyes opened much, much wider than I had ever imagined, even though we didn't manage to explore much of the town of Port Said.

It was similar in Aden, the small area of Yemen that for 20 some years after 1937 was ruled as a British Crown Colony. We called there and were able to leave the ship, but with very strict instructions and protection against moving very far. The Colony was only 192 square miles in total, but as far as we were concerned it was almost limited to a stroll, before we arrived at a specific point where the Military Police were stationed to insist we turned back for our own safety. Once again, we were left without any understanding as to why there were strong feelings against English soldiers.

The experiences were different, but just as shattering of pre-conceived ideas, as we stopped at Colombo and Singapore. Both were large bustling ports and wonderful cities with great buildings, busy streets, markets and shops to rival anything I had seen and, in the case of Singapore, a beautifully laid out city centre with wide boulevards and open spaces. I am now told that soon afterwards 'modernisation came' and the things I loved, as in the photo on the next page, have long since gone! Hong Kong had an entirely different character. It was Asian in looks and feel, though we did not stop long enough for there to be much time ashore.

The final part of this transforming journey came after we left Pusan [now Busan], and the Royal Norfolk regiment and many of the other specialist service people had left the ship. No more than 30 or 40 of us were left to continue to Kure, the Japanese port. The most surprising fact was that a guard had to be provided! It had been a feature of the whole voyage but I had not been aware of it, for the guarding was entirely undertaken by the Norfolks. But now the remaining number of us were assigned by the Daily Orders to guard duty. It was absolutely necessary because, as we found out, one poor fellow was in 'clink', a small bare space in the very nose of the ship, for some misdemeanour he had committed. Whilst not assigned to have any dealings directly with him, we had to ensure that he couldn't escape!

St Andrews Cathedral, Singapore

11. Why a Korean War?

As a sixth form student, in the days when the only ways news reached our family were via the BBC radio news at 1 and 6 pm and my father's daily News Chronicle newspaper, the Korean peninsula and events concerning it were somewhat sparse. Most people now will be aware of, and concerned about, North Korea's regime and their capability to fire nuclear weapons. Perhaps a majority will be aware of the successful Korean electronics manufacturers Samsung; the country's car production as the fifth largest in the world with Hyundai, Kia, SsangYong and Daewoo as the best known South Korean manufacturers, in what is now considered to be a very thriving economy. However, I suspect that even today the majority are not really clear as to how the 'Forgotten War' came about. So here is a short account of Korean recent history from my personal research, utilising the online courses provided by Professor Kim of Seoul University.

The geographic location is important, for the Korean peninsula extends for 684 miles into the Pacific Ocean south from China towards Japan, and is surrounded by the Sea of Japan on the East and the Yellow Sea on the West. The Eastern part of the peninsula is mountainous with the Paektu Mountains of which the highest peak is at 9003 feet. The land area is some 85,270 square miles and in 2013 had a population of 74.5 million. As the peninsula is now divided into two separate countries it needs to be recognised that they have different geographical and socio-economic characteristics, for the current North Korea has much less agriculture than the present South Korea, due to their different topography. The two countries did not and do not now have similar sized populations. There are 24.72 million people in the North but

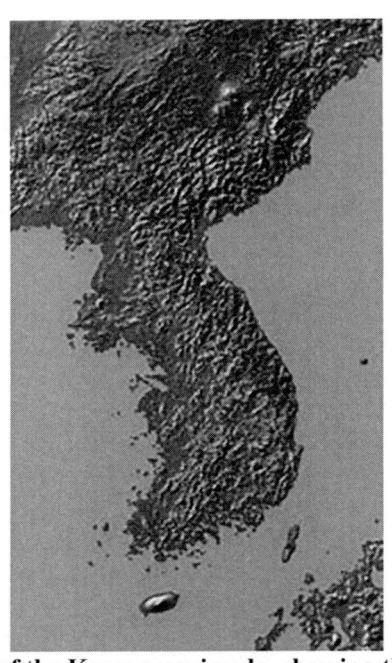

Geography of the Korean peninsula, showing the high land

The configuration of powers in the Far East

48.96 million in South Korea, for whilst the North is the larger area by a fifth, it is much more mountainous. There are other wide disparities between North and South, with people in the North having a disposable GDP of $1,800, whilst people in the South have $32,400; likewise, infant mortality in the North is 26.21 per 1,000 births against the 4.08 per 1,000 in the South. The military capabilities of the two countries are also very different, with 1.19 million on active service in the North and only 0.65 million in the South. Their military expenditure reverses these trends with the South spending $26.1 billion as against the North's $8.2 billion in 2008, though this accounted for some 22.3% of North Korea's GDP against 2.8% of GDP in the South.

Historically, the earliest known Korean artefacts date to around 8000BC. In the earliest times, the peninsula was not divided as now, though by the 1st century BC included Manchuria and formed three kingdoms that were united into one only in 676 AD. In 1392, the Josean Dynasty ruled and their King Sejon the Great, in the 15th century, introduced reforms to the administrative, social, and economic systems, as well as introducing the Hangul alphabet. All these were based on Buddhist principles. Between 1440 and 1560, there were migrations to the northern provinces, designed to strengthen the border. This created a society of mixed backgrounds without either an aristocracy or long-standing religious institutions. However, it did have a strong and ambitious merchant class, as well as a strong military tradition. Local elites gained administrative positions and adopted Confucian literati lifestyles, but were not able to attain the highest-level positions.

From the 16th century, the Josean Dynasty ruled as a royal house, but faced foreign invasions, internal power struggles and rebellions. The dynasty largely managed to keep power by military means, supported by China. They also kept a strict isolationist policy to all except China. By the 19th century, failure to modernise linked to China's economic weakness, led to foreign powers ruling the peninsula until Japan defeated China, in 1897. From then until 1910 a brief period of independence, known as the Korean Empire, followed. The state was in fact dominated by Russia, and when Japan defeated Russia, they forced Korea to sign a protectorate treaty. In 1910, Japan annexed the Korean Empire.

For the next 40 years Japan ruled, and their primary interest was in the raw materials that were available in Korea and, to a greater extent, in Manchuria, to which Korea is a natural gateway. Korea was thus a colonial subject nation controlled by the Japanese as the ruling authority. During the Japanese colonial rule, the north became the more industrial region of Korea and became highly receptive to Protestant missionaries, who brought Western knowledge, hospitals, schools, and a window to the wider world. The middle-class elites sent their sons to the Protestant schools and in turn the sons often became strong nationalists, who saw the United States as their rallying point in opposition to Japanese colonial imperialism. In spite of this, in the North, the machinery of government was Japanese, with them controlling the schools' education, the police and the armed forces. In the south, Korean hierarchy developed, because of their powerful landowners of large estates, who developed relatively harmonious relationships with the Japanese overlords, and similarly with those accepting and accepted Koreans, who were selected and trained as teachers, police or members of the armed forces. But to the vast majority of Korean people, it was a harsh regime that brooked no resistance to its wishes.

Naturally some desired an independent Korean nation and were able to establish a Provisional Government of the Republic of Korea in exile, based in Shanghai, China. Armed resistance movements developed which the Provisional Government coordinated against the Japanese, culminating in the formation, in 1940, of the Korean Liberation Army, bringing together many of the resistance groups. Then came the 1939–45 war, bringing to an end the forty years of heavy handed Japanese colonial rule.

The development of the atomic bomb and the sudden deployment, without any warning, of two against Japan "designed to deliver a colossal shock, not only to the Japanese people but also to the leaders of the Soviet Union"[4], clearly shortened the conflict. But this was not the only shock to the Japanese military and political leaders, for, on the 9th August 1945, 1.5 million Russian soldiers attacked Japan's northernmost outpost, Manchuria, across a land front of more than 2,000 miles. "This was the last great military operation of the Second World War."[5]

These two almost simultaneous events led to the ceasefire and capitulation of Japan in August 1945, though not to any acceptance of their brutality for "… their political, educational and corporate leaders … still seek to excuse, and even to ennoble, the actions of their parents and grandparents, so many of whom forsook humanity in favour of a perversion of honour and an aggressive nationalism which should properly be recalled with shame."[6] Such a judgement can also apply to years of brutal rule over the Korean peninsula.

Yet Japan's abrupt capitulation was one of the most celebrated moments in Korean history, presenting Koreans with the opportunity to form their own independent nation. But there was little time for celebration due to the immediate problem of controlling and ruling the country. There were 700,000 Japanese in Korea, who needed to be repatriated, and vast numbers of Korean people who had been displaced from their places of origin and affinity, all requiring considerable re-settlement plans and programmes; the position of the USSR, and Stalin in particular, was uncertain, as was the potential role of China, also recovering from Japanese rule and divided between the Nationalists and Communists. Thus much of the actual events happened by circumstance rather than by careful planning. In fact, Korea was soon divided into Soviet and American occupation zones. This was almost by happenstance or coincidence, for there was no historical justification for the division of Korea, or the 38th parallel being the dividing line between North and South. It was

---

[4] Max Hastings, *Nemesis: The Battle for Japan 1944–45*, Harper 2007, *p.518*
[5] ibid, *p. 525*
[6] ibid, *p. 598*

apparently drawn, without much forethought, by a couple of young officers in the American army! When the 38th parallel was proposed to the Soviets, the Americans had no idea if they would accept. Surprisingly though, the Soviets halted their advance at the 38th parallel, and thus began the division of Korea.

There remains considerable debate among historians as to the major influences on the developments in the Korean peninsula. Was it, on the one hand, the United States joining the Allies in the 1939–45 war and the wider Southern Asian geo-political considerations of the great powers, or the attempts, by Koreans, to develop an independent nation that were the major influences and the determining factors in the future development of the Korean Peninsula? There remains debate as to the nature of the moves and counter moves of the great powers in the following decade, and the exact strengths or weaknesses of the local figures.

The first major event was a conference held in December 1945, in Moscow, which established a Joint Commission that met numerous times throughout 1946, to discuss how to establish a unified provisional government, as a trusteeship for the peninsula. Yet the actual policies on the ground, by the military occupants, moved quickly towards division shortly after liberation, for both the Soviets and Americans formed separate advisory and administrative bodies in Seoul and Pyongyang immediately upon their arrival. This did not prevent a joint agreement to withdraw all occupying forces, and that happened in 1948–49.

A key figure among those who resisted the Japanese during their occupation was Syngman Rhee (1875–1965). Living in Hawaii, he was an ardent, strong personality, firmly committed to his principles but dominating others. He became the first President of the exiled Provisional Government from 1919 to 1939. He naturally had opponents but was the one nationalist leader who was well known to the United States authorities and was the most prominent and powerful of the leading Korean personnel. Once he purged all moderate elements and took over the Representative Democratic

Council in the spring of 1947, the path was set for a separate southern government. The US asked the newly founded United Nations to form the United Nations Temporary Commission on Korea, to supervise a Korean Constitutional Assembly election in May 1948 and the process led to the establishment of the Republic of Korea in August 15, 1948. The Constitutional Assembly elected Syngnam Rhee, who was unopposed, to become the first president of the Republic of Korea. The USSR refused to participate in this UN sponsored election because they controlled an area of Korea that was far smaller in population than that controlled by the US. The Soviets quickly responded to these moves and held their own separate elections on August 25, 1948 which inaugurated the Democratic People's Republic of Korea in the north.

The nature of the Korean society in 1945 was, as Professor Kim has written, "Korean society itself was split into different groups, classes, and political ideologies. On one side were elite groups, like landlords and industrialists and many who had collaborated with the Japanese and maintained special privileges throughout the colonial period. The right also included those who served in the Japanese state as policemen or bureaucrats. But on the other hand, the left was composed of students, intellectuals, peasants, and workers who often had strong sympathies to Communism.

The extent to which we can divide Korean society into these two categories may be questioned as probably most people did not have any political affiliations. But in general, we can divide the interactions of the immediate post-liberation years into these two groups. And what's interesting is that regardless of one's position, most Koreans favoured a somewhat socialist platform of state ownership of key industries and a generous social welfare agenda."

Thus we can see something of the nature of the real politics of these two countries, with the irreconcilable people and parties and the deadly politic of assassination that developed. Although the negotiations to unify the two Koreas continued throughout 1945–1947, in many ways the movement towards separate states started quite early, and the path became hardened through violence. Syngman Rhee emerged in the South and Kim Il-Sung in the North as the most powerful and influential leaders, because so many of their rivals had been systematically eliminated during the violence of the immediate post-liberation years and, later, the Korean War. In effect, an entire generation of Korean leadership had perished during the struggle to establish the Korean nation after the end of Japanese rule in 1945.

The reality was a divided nation, each party looking to a great power, either Soviet Russia or the United States of America, for support, that neither seemed prepared to offer. In 1950, the USA made its position clear – it too was interested in Korea. This appears to have provided Stalin with the encouragement to discuss with Kim Il-Sung and the Chinese a strategy for seizing opportunities in Southeast Asia, beginning with North Korea invading South Korea. Whilst perhaps of little geo-political import, that blatant action crossed the 38th parallel, a boundary agreed by the United Nations, and "appeared to challenge the entire structure of post-war collective security."[7] Thus the Korean War became a United Nations reality.

---

[7] John L Gaddis *'The Cold War: A New History'* Penguin 2005 p.4

12. Japan

So often, during this period of National Service, there was an upside to what appeared to be unnecessary, inconvenient and petty chores, and for me I found it on the ship's deck at dawn. We were then sailing through the Japanese Inland Sea, with islands covered in trees and vegetation scattered around the vista. The islands seemed to be substantial mounds of vegetation sprouting out of the water. The only sign of human life or occupation were a few groups of small houses clustered around a beach. It was a beautiful morning with a clear blue sky as the sun rose and cast its sparkling brilliant rays across the smooth water. It was, and remains, a most magical experience with a unique, to me, blue sea of such a hue that I have never seen again, and the dark treed islands showing the different greens shading into browns, and setting off the whole amazing sight. This on-duty guard stood in the silence of a large ship, slowly and steadily proceeding through the water, and took in a view that is as fresh a memory now as it was a vision then. Kure, our destination port, was a large natural harbour that contained a small but busy port. Its significance then or now is hard to gauge, for no Japanese person I have since met had even heard of it! But it seemed a fair sized town, with an active port so far as we were able to judge. In one sense, this was a limited opportunity to explore or get to know Japan or the Japanese people, for visiting, meeting or talking with any local people was forbidden by a strict non- fraternisation regime that was in force and enforced by the Military Police.

Aerial view of today's Kure port and town

One surprise was to see, when I walked down the main street, at the busy road junction, a policeman standing on a small round podium in the middle of the junction directing all the traffic, by hand signals and by blowing a whistle. He was in absolute control and woe betide you if you dared to imagine that there was a sufficient gap in the traffic flow to allow you possibly to cross, and so step on to the road. That whistle would shrilly sound and appear not to stop, and the policeman would point his outstretched arm – at me – and all the traffic seemed to halt. Whether it actually did or not is immaterial, for the experience was so sudden, unexpected and shattering, even frightening, that I only ever did it once! I don't think local people ever succumbed to the temptation. On one Saturday morning, where normally the police officer stood on his podium, there was a youngster, in police cadet uniform, on the podium and directing all the traffic, with all the authority and confidence of the usual officers. It was a safe and apparently flawless performance, watched, to assess the performance, by a couple of senior police officers. It seemed a very practical and effective way to provide an 'apprenticeship' for potential police officers.

Our transit camp was on the edge of the town and virtually surrounded by farmed paddy fields. Of more immediate concern to us was that we were at home again in the Nissen type huts, exactly like the ones left behind on Salisbury Plain, except that these were all raised about four foot high on stilts.

As a transit camp, there were minimal facilities, apparent army organisation or activity. Many people came and left within a few days, but I stayed for almost four months. There was a small office with a few clerks, who produced and displayed Daily Orders. The first building as one entered the camp was a guardhouse, with soldiers always on duty, but little else like normal barracks in the UK. On the whole, we are left free and able to come and go as we pleased.

Whilst there, I met up with the Inspector Gunner whose responsibilities included Korea. He came and went there frequently. As I had never been properly assessed as a Technical Assistant, it seemed important, both to him and me, that this should be accomplished. For a number of weeks, I was notionally on a course, but whether anything happened was a matter of 'luck rather than good management', as my mother used to say to me. The so called course was never structured sufficiently for me to be 'qualified' as a Tech Ack.

Somehow, the details of which are unclear to me now, and probably were then, I, with a driver, took an officer to some destination out in the countryside, in a Jeep, as he was about his business. It was part of a process to further my learning to drive, and was an uneventful experience except for one incident. It was acceptable to the officer that I drove and he sat in the passenger seat and gave instructions, whilst the driver sat in the back. All went well, even in a small village, where I stopped to allow kimono-clad ladies to back out of a home and cross the street to their own home, walking backward and bowing every few yards to the friend they had just left. None were mown down! But as we left one hamlet and I accelerated away, we approached a narrow bridge across a small river. The bridge was set at an angle to the road necessitating a fairly sharp left turn, then go over the bridge, and a similar right turn after crossing the small bridge. As we approached the officer said,

"Right, change down now for this bridge."

It might have been better had he not spoken, for I did exactly as he commanded and moved the gear stick DOWN from the physically higher position to one lower, changing in fact into top gear, in the process! The Jeep shot forward at a very increased speed, rather than slowed as was expected, but I managed to negotiate the bridge in safety, crossing it and also staying on the road. Having made the error, I felt it was a brilliant bit of driving, but Mr Officer thought otherwise and commanded me to stop, let me have a piece of his mind and informed me that he required me to move to the back seat and, for his own safety and peace of mind, the driver to assume his proper responsibilities. Perhaps unsurprisingly, as this was a piece of unauthorised behaviour, nothing more was heard of the matter!

Because their work base was next to where I was supposed to be undergoing a course, I spent some time with the broadcasters on the local Forces Network. I was both interested and fascinated at their work, gathering news, interviewing people and putting it together for broadcasting. I would have loved to remain with them and become part of their set up but that wasn't possible and has remained a small matter of regret that this time never materialised into a more valuable opportunity.

Whilst there I did have to undertake one guard duty, not in the Transit Camp itself but in another building in the heart of Kure. Many British soldiers caught one or other venereal disease whilst abroad. Whilst we were in Japan, associating with Japanese people and visiting them in their homes was strictly forbidden. Thus, for some who made friends with Japanese girls, sexual activity carried army penalties. The guard duty was in one facility, part hospital, part treatment centre, part prison. On the one duty I undertook there, it was soon obvious that the NCO guard commander, unknown to us, did this duty regularly and was on reasonable terms with some of the inmates. I found it highly suspicious! That suspicion was confirmed when I was told, about 0100 hrs, to accompany one prisoner to the toilet in a nearby block. Between each block there were covered walkways, and as we progressed, me walking slightly behind him, he suddenly jumped the low wall and ran towards the perimeter. I followed, caught him and returned with him to the room in which he was being held. Little was said by the guard commander and I was allowed to go to sleep, but before I did so, I could hear the commander and the prisoner muttering together. A couple of hours later I was woken and told to repeat the exercise. I was obviously even more watchful and held his arm to the toilet. On the return journey, he turned, tried to knock me down and hared off as before. Again, I followed and was catching him up when he came to a building, the corner of which was a yard or less from the perimeter fence. He disappeared round the building and I followed – but he had stopped, was waiting for me, punched me, knocking me down, ran to the corner of the fence and was up and over before I could catch him. It was obvious that a car was waiting below to take him away. The guard commander asked for no details or full account, but simply told me that I was placed on a charge and could go to bed! I did and slept well. At breakfast time, I was taken, as a prisoner, to another building and locked up until transport came and took me back to the transit camp. There I was hauled before the CO, to whom I gave a full account of what had happened. He looked at me hard and long before replying,

"Very strange. I shall need to look into this matter further."

The NCO who had marched me into the CO's office, then asked,

"Is he to be kept in custody, sir?"

After a slight pause, the CO replied,

"No, that won't be necessary."

and turning to me said,

"I shall no doubt need to see you again, so you had better remain available."

I heard no more and was not recalled to see the CO again. So, a couple of days later I saw the Chief Clerk and asked,

"Am I still expecting to see the CO again?"

"No, you're not. You're in the clear. It's others who are being investigated."

I assumed that, of the guard that night, the commander decided that I was the softie, who could be relied upon to not cause too much trouble. In so far as the prisoner got away, I suppose he was right – but I doubt if he got away with it!

What did happen in my time in the camp was that the Chaplain and I met, and when he discovered that I was a candidate for ordination he suggested that I should work with and for him. He sought permission and it was granted, and I officially became Chaplain's Assistant. The idea was that I should take the opportunity to study, but it didn't seem to be very effective! Each morning I would walk out of the camp and into a neighbouring camp, where the church was located, and I had the freedom to use the office cum vestry at the back. Whether the Chaplain would be there seemed haphazard, in fact, I never had any idea what he did. Nor was I ever aware of any services held in the camp church and did not attend any. I had more contact with the Japanese handyman/gardener than the chaplain, and in some ways that was much more interesting, but not productive of study.

With all the problems of language differences, we did manage to communicate and it was useful to be able to try to make some sense of the life he was now living and what they had been through during and after the war.

Church activities, throughout the stay in Kure, were in a church much nearer the port than our camp, and that was part of the Australian contingent's camp and married quarters. As Australia had been part of the Eastern theatre of war, they had some responsibilities, under General MacArthur, for the government of Japan. Theirs was a more permanent camp with resident families and therefore an active church life, more like what was familiar to us in Britain. I joined the choir and was able to meet with others, including Japanese, of a similar age to myself. From one of the Japanese young women, I was able to hear something of the horror of what it had been like to be at the receiving end of the atomic bomb dropped on Hiroshima. The descriptions of the mutilations suffered by some people who were brought to the hospital in Kure were indeed harrowing. She also showed me some very sharp language skill as I pressed her to find what her occupation was. Her reply was,

"I'm only an interrupter!"

She was, of course, an interpreter – and her reply no doubt stayed within the bounds of her confidentiality contract.

Choir practice one night led to one of the most frightening experiences of my service. As we went to the church, it was raining heavily and by the time we left there were storm conditions that were confirmed as a tornado. The bus skirted the shore of the harbour and there were usually small boats moored there. This night they were dark shapes jumping all over the place. Then we all heard a piercing scream. The driver stopped the bus, the screaming frantically continued, so the driver began to move the bus in order for the headlights to scan the water. The scene was pandemonium, there was nothing that any of could see, but the screaming continued, and eventually the driver proceeded on his route and to call and inform the authorities. To show how bad this storm was, when I arrived back in the camp, I had to wade through water to reach my hut. Just after midnight we were woken because the water had risen to the top of the steps, some four feet, and we had to be prepared to evacuate the hut if it rose higher. It didn't, but only slowly subsided.

As I have said, fraternising with the Japanese was forbidden, but there were some necessities in which we did meet with some. Having a haircut was one, and there were facilities for us and Japanese hairdressers. There was little difference regarding the haircut, but once the cutting was over, a massage was given. Steaming towels were placed round the neck and shoulder, and then the area was massaged, gently but firmly, and it always ended with the masseur/ hairdresser bringing the edge of both hands rapidly up and down on the whole of the shoulders in rapid succession. It was amazing, felt fantastic and we always walked out feeling a million dollars!

Finally, as Christmas drew near, I was asked to call into the camp office one morning. When I did so, I was asked if I could type and, in response to my non-committal response indicating that I had messed around on my father's typewriter, I was further challenged,

"But you must, you're the Chaplain's assistant."

Yes, I argued, not knowing what all this was about, but there's not much typing involved in that. There was some puzzlement on the part of those present but this was solved when the senior among them said,

"Well, there's no one else that fits the bill, so you'll have to go."

With that I was informed that I would be leaving that evening, well about 0200 hrs, to fly to Seoul in Korea to join the 1903 Air Observation Flight as senior clerk! Not the vast impersonal machine that disposed of soldiers at will, but another way of dealing with things that was just as inefficient!

As with most other strange things in this army, there was nothing that I could do about it other than set about packing and following the arrangements that were made for me to sleep in the Guardroom corridor, so as not to disturb anyone else when I had to leave on the transport.

War torn Seoul in 1950

13. Finally – Korea

Comfort was not one of the attributes of the army in the 1950s. So, after an uncomfortable and restless three or four hours in the Guardroom corridor, I was rudely shaken to be driven through the darkness to Hiroshima airport. There I joined a few others and took my 'seat' on a transport aeroplane, for my first ever flight. As a transport plane, it was empty but for sacks of mail and boxes of equipment and other material. The mail sacks were set at the sides and became our seats for the journey. It wasn't too bad and half-asleep we journeyed on. We woke up as we approached Seoul, for the wireless became busy. There was some problem, and after discussion between the pilot and Air Traffic Control, we had no other option but to circle round and re-approach for landing. The same thing happened again, and once more we climbed up and went around the circle, and again approached for landing. How many times we did that I have no memory, though I still remember the queasiness I felt in the stomach and the throbbing headache and general sense of dizziness. It was a renewal of the discovery when crossing the Bay of Biscay, that I am not the best of travellers!

Eventually we landed and no account was taken of any feelings or sickness that I or others felt, we were simply processed and taken to the Transit Camp in the city. I later discovered that, at that time, the Seoul authorities had banned any development that did not conform to the traditional style of building. The Transit camp was such a traditional and old building, and it did not take a practised eye to assess that the conditions were disgusting. There was nothing in the way of convenience, with limited toilets and washing facilities and nowhere for anyone to go to sit down or relax. Transit camps are inevitably places of inactivity as people wait for instructions, transport, arrangements or decisions to be made for and about them. That day we were relatively fortunate, for somehow someone discovered that there was a three-tonne truck returning to Divisional HQ, and so a few of us could be accommodated on it and with minor diversions we could all be delivered to our respective destinations. Out of the city there were no roads but only dirt tracks and, whilst the one to Divisional HQ was in reasonable shape, not all the places where the passengers had to go were on the main road. So, we journeyed twisting and turning to avoid ditches or potholes, bouncing around in the back of this great truck as if we were in free flight. Naturally, I was the final passenger to be delivered, for 1903 Air OP Flight, to which I was destined, was located just over the hill from Divisional HQ, the driver's destination.

The driver pulled to the roadside and shouted that this was my destination. Carrying my kit, I walked into the camp that had tents seemingly randomly scattered around, and although it was as quiet as the proverbial graveyard, eventually someone spotted and me.

"Hello, can I help you?"

"I am reporting for duty, sir," I replied.

"Ah, right. It's good to have you with us, though I wasn't aware that we are expecting anybody at the moment. So, what's your name?"

"7287 Gunner Hutchinson, sir."

"And what's your job, Hutchinson?"

"I'm a trained Technical Assistant, sir, but I understand I am here as a Senior Clerk."

"Ah, that's good for we need one of those. Well, you're welcome and you've come at just the right time. There is no one else about at the moment because they are all in the dining tent, over there, having a meal. Perhaps it would be best if you went and joined them now, had a meal and then we can sort out where you are to sleep and so on. So, shall I take you across there?"

"No, thank you, sir, I couldn't face anything to eat at present."

"Oh, why not, are you alright?"

"I'm not feeling too good, sir, I've been up since 0200 hrs, flown from Japan in an uncomfortable flight being flung around sitting on a mailbag, circled round until I felt as sick as a parrot, and then landed at Seoul and taken to view the shameful conditions of the transit camp, and finally sat in the back of a three-tonne truck, bounced up and down and round about to get here, and I'm not feeling too good, Sir, and certainly couldn't eat anything."

"Are you sure? That's a great pity for it's an excellent meal tonight. I think Cook is practising for Christmas Day and I hear there is chicken, roast potatoes and all the trimmings. Are you quite sure you don't want any of that?"

"Yes, sir!"

"Right. Well we'd better find somewhere for you to sleep to tonight. There's room in my crew's tent and they won't mind you bunking with them for a bit. So, I'll show where to go and then I'll clear it with the crew. Come on."

So, he organised me a bed in a tent with some space, and I fell on to it. I was only half awake at best when the usual occupants came home to find an extra body, virtually dead to the world and grumpy into the bargain, on a bed that hadn't been there before. Such were the logistical and caring arrangements the army made for its serving soldiers in a battle zone in 1951. As I fell asleep, it was with thoughts of the majesty of the War Office, with all its machinations, that had moved me twice, the second time taking me from a locally chosen path that would have excited and motivated me, to deposit me in a transit camp where no one knew who I was, why I was there or what use I might be – for I still remained a Technical Assistant who had never finished a proper training course, even though the CO and School of Artillery thought I could be an Inspector Gunner – but I had played around on my dad's typewriter!!

I add, at this point, that the Christmas meal was the stupendous food festivity that the officer had suggested. Everyone was there and all apart from the officers were seated at the tables. Keeping to the age old tradition, as I understood it, the officers waited upon and served us. Not only was the food splendid, but there were crackers to be pulled and silly jokes shared. It was an isolated island of time when the machinations of a forces unit were almost laid aside, and we all became a group of folk, thrown together by circumstances way beyond our control and even understanding, and for this brief time became human beings sharing our circumstances together. We were all far from home, we had families, friends, girlfriends, wives or sweethearts that we longed to be with, and for a moment we wrapped it all up together, relaxed in each other's company and had some fun. It was good.

14. What Is an Air Op Flight?

I had some vague idea about Air OP Flights once I was commanded to set off to join one but, looking around, there wasn't much to tell me more. A dirt track led from the 'road' and on the right was a command post truck with awnings round it and a sandbagged entrance. One or two other small tents and a large marquee, that served as the dining and meeting room, and at least two middle sized tents that it was hard to determine what they were. There were also one or two other small tents. To the left of the track were five marquees, each with a small plane standing somewhere near, and there was a flat area with a wind sock at one end. Clearly it was the landing strip for the small planes! In addition to the planes' crews to maintain each aircraft, the rest of the personnel were from the Royal Artillery, except the two cooks! We had our own transport, mainly three-tonne trucks, Land Rovers and Jeeps, with their drivers and maintenance staff, all of whom were nominally under the direction of our QMS, Sergeant Jed.

But being a Technical Assistant, I knew that, whilst I and all other Teck Acks could set about mapping the exact location of the artillery guns and the target they were to aim at so that the gunners could set each 25 pounder accurately, it would not be enough to ensure that shells sent to that target would arrive there. We did not have that precision. Wind and weather conditions would affect each shell and we couldn't account for those. Hence the need for an Observer, usually a senior officer, who would position himself, on a hill or a tall house, in such a way that he could see the target and the shells as they landed. He would then control the guns and the further rounds they fired, with instructions to increase or decrease the distance a few feet or move to left or right by a degree or so. It was the only way we knew.

Later research showed that during the 1939–45 war at least one RAF squadron had been established, of which 1903 Flight had been one, in which light aircraft would be piloted by artillery officers trained for the purpose, so that they could fly above the target area and direct the accurate firing of the guns. They had been used in a number of war zones and seemed to have proved their value in both Borneo and Malaya. Flights had been disbanded or resurrected, but there seems always to have been an active one somewhere. It seems that 1903 Flight had been used in Malaya and then transferred to Hong Kong, from where the majority of the RAF personnel I knew in 1951–1952 had come. The records are not clear and what their purpose was in Hong Kong seems not now to be known, for the records show that 1903 Flight was only brought to life again in October 1951, to transfer to Korea and serve the Commonwealth Division there.

So here were five Auster light planes with five RA officers, four British and one Australian, one to each plane, which they would pilot into the unknown territory of the enemy and gently fly around when the guns were firing, naturally keeping away from the flight of the shells, but near enough to see both the target and the exploding shells, and from there control the further firing of the guns. These five would do that for any of the artillery guns of the Commonwealth or American Divisions that had responded to the United Nations determination to control the activities of Northern Korea and protect the southern part of that peninsula.

It was, as I soon came to understand, an awesomely complex task. Facing us were not just North Korean but Chinese troops, equipped with Soviet guns who operated in a fashion unlike anything two world wars had shown. Their front-line soldiers dug trenches in which to protect themselves in some meagre fashion against whatever onslaughts they faced. Here these Chinese troops had taken that technique one step further – they dug tunnels, unseen from land or air, in which they lived and from which they attacked. Their artillery guns were deep underground, but were able to be moved to the camouflaged surface, fire their round and retreat again, leaving little sign of where they were or what they had done. There was no way that opposing artillery could track or respond to such hidden weapons.

The pilots of these five flimsy aircraft were thus not limited to controlling artillery that knew its target, but were used, in two-hour stints, to traverse the skies above the North Korean lines in the hope that they would spot disturbed ground, any unusual topographical feature, a minute sign of human habitation or life, or some other feature that had simply not been seen before. These would be reported, even filmed on another flight, so that they could be analysed and understood. All this in wooded, hilly territory where an unpractised eye spotted nothing. The one time, on a sunny summer morning, when I was given the experience by one of our pilots, I, the queasy traveller at best, was so bored and uncomfortable that I went to sleep as one of our pilots took me with him. There was no surprise that I was faced with a sardonic but disgusted pilot when we landed, but my untrained eyes could see nothing unusual or different on the land below – hence the boredom.

One of the integral functions of 1903 Flight was to photograph the terrain north of the 38th parallel. To do this each plane could be fitted with a camera in the nose. It could be of enormous value in the circumstances in which the UN Division operated, where the North Korean or Chinese guns were hidden underground for, if a photograph could be obtained of the moment their gun was fired, there was at least the possibility of determining an accurate grid reference point. 1903 Flight also had a photographer, a reservist, who had set up his own photographic business in the UK, but that did not prevent him being recalled. When I arrived, he had an adapted three-tonne truck in which to live and operate. Many photos had to be sent onward for further examination, and he would ensure that their quality was of the highest standard.

He was something of an entrepreneur with an eye to his UK business, for he was able to send some photographs to the Illustrated London News and have them accepted for publication. Some were no longer newsworthy by the time they reached the editor, but I saw his letters explaining this. Firm evidence of the quality of his work. One day he came to Peter S, my fellow clerk, and me, and said,

"I've just been reading that there is a newly designed all-singing-and-dancing photographic workshop truck. It's got an up to the minute dark room and is full of all the facilities I need. I wish we had one here for me to use."

Peter S and I looked at each other, and I replied,

"Well, we don't know if we could get one, probably not, but we could try."

He became excited and, with the enthusiastic professional's rhapsody, he explained all the advantages that having one would give. So, I said,

"Have you got the reference details, its number and so on?"

He had, enabling us to look it up and set about composing a signal which, for proper etiquette, was shown to the CO, and sent off to the War Office Supplies Dept. with a copy to SE Asia HQ.

Peter S, with much more experience and understanding of the proper channels through which things had to be indented for, especially if they were new, was sceptical, and foresaw that we would have the signal returned from HQ, probably with a telling off. As each day came and went, such a withering response never arrived, and we relaxed and came to the alternative view that nothing would come of the request. It was bound to have been lost in the arcane mysteries of the War Office by some junior clerk. A few weeks went by before the unit's office erupted with two Peter's dancing for joy. We had been allocated one! It was already on its way! We even had a date on which it was expected to arrive. We also had a photographer who was over the moon with ecstatic joy when we told him.

Unfortunately, there was a repercussion when the day came and the vehicle arrived. No one had thought to tell us, and we hadn't thought about how this machinery was to be powered!! A generator should have been ordered at the same time, to go with it. Without it was useless. However, we had no doubt that, with our fulsome signal to HQ explaining that 'they' had omitted to send a vital part of the equipment, we would have one within a few days.

The Auster planes were looked after by RAF teams of technicians, one to each plane, who repaired, serviced, monitored and, I suspect, loved these craft so that they were always airworthy and ready for the regular daily tour of duty. As with all RAF planes, a daily report on their condition was made and wired to HQ and the Air Ministry, and these provided the information as to whether the plane was serviceable or not. If it wasn't, it was the ways and means by which spare parts and replacements were provided. It was a most efficient way to ensure each plane was serviceable or, if not, quickly enabling it to return to serviceable duty. This was the only bit of my national service experience that seemed to be efficient and to work. It even extended to the personal level, for each RAF technician was monitored and could be required, by HQ command, to attend courses that were judged to be necessary for their current competence or future progression. When this happened, of course, no transport was provided for whoever was required to attend a course. So, we had RAF Technicians setting off for Hong Kong or Singapore, to make their own way there and back. None found it difficult flying from one airport to another, and all seemed to arrive on time for the start of the course and return within an acceptable timescale.

15. Daily Life by the Imjin River

Life in 1903 Air OP Flight was, on the whole, relaxed and pleasant. Perhaps this was largely so because the officers kept themselves to themselves and did not mix in any way with anyone other than the crew of RAF technicians with whom each one worked. Inevitably the pilots and their crews grew together to some extent, for the lives of the pilots rested with their crews. Each team developed their own team behaviour, to which no others could be party. But there was no fraternisation, nor indeed opportunity for it, between pilot and crew outside the strict confines of their work. The rest of us were unaware of the officers' duties or flights, other than by seeing planes take off and return. To an innocent observer, they seemed to lounge about for most of the day. It seems to be the natural reaction of all pilots of aircraft when not in the air flying, and for these men it was time to recover from the danger they faced, the considerable skills they needed and the stress each day brought to them.

In one sense it seems, looking back, that it was surprisingly so relaxed for us because our office was 'built' round the CO's office-cum-command post and at one end was the location of the wireless operators and their equipment. The wireless network, operated by Command Headquarters, covered all the artillery units of the Commonwealth and United States Divisions. We were located over the hill from the headquarters, who often lost connectivity with the network, leaving us as the senior outstation, to assume the 'command' role and relay any orders, given to us by phone, to the whole network. So, there were wireless messages coming and going all day long as we worked, and we were aware of how things were operating day by day. It was not uncommon, as the topography was not very helpful to radio communications, for HQ to ring up and say that they were having difficulties, so we would now be Senior Outstation, and messages from senior officers would be passed to us by telephone for us to relay on to all the units. In one sense, it was helpful to us in that the radio operators were on duty throughout the day and night, so we always had someone in the office, and thus never missed a telephone call. It was also pleasant on those occasions when, because it was very, very cold, or there was something to celebrate, we would get the message to be transmitted,

"Six, and all stations six, splice the main brace!"

For this simple soul, I thought that this custom was an old fashioned Naval practise that had long since ceased to operate. Not so! Peter S and I would soon pass the message around, one going officially to tell QMS Jed, whilst the other circulated round the camp. Soon there would be a long queue outside the QMS store as he dispensed the statutory tot of rum. Being teetotal it never interested me, though I always claimed my ration in order to give it someone else.

There were times when we could relax, for there were days, or at least hours, when no planes could take off and operate due to the weather and operational necessity. In the summer, all flights were either very early, around dawn, or later, as dusk fell, because it would have been almost an open invitation to be shot at and so too dangerous to fly over enemy lines in clear blue skies. On such summer afternoons, by some osmotic signal, most of us, who were not required to work, would set off down to the river that almost bordered our camp site and runway. There we would swim, relax and have some fun together.

It's amazing, in the circumstances of our lives, that other aspects were managed with little fuss or impact. If we were ill, there were medical facilities and each one would make their way there and be treated. I suffered an abscess in my mouth and clearly needed to have it dealt with. So, a vehicle and driver was detailed to take me to the dentist. The driver knew where to go and how to get there on the tracks and paths that managed as minor roads, and I had no doubt we would get there. The dentist, having examined me, was quite clear that one tooth would have to be taken out. This would be done without anaesthetic but I must have an injection. It was the best one ever! The medical orderly who gave it to me chose my buttock, asked me to drop my trousers and then saying,

"Two smart taps."

He did indeed tap me twice – and that was it! It was a different matter with the dentist who, while I sat in his chair, poked and prodded and intensely worked away, with only some minor discomfort for me – apparently. Suddenly, he stood back for a short breather, and breaking his concentration, took a look at me.

"Oh, my goodness,"

he said,

"you look terrible. I'm so sorry that I have been too occupied to notice. We'll have to stop and let you recover a bit."

With that I was taken off and put into a bed and made to stay there for a while before he judged I was capable of undergoing the remainder the treatment. I was sore on the journey back and had the remainder of the day off – but it was effective in clearing the abscess. Thank goodness!

16. Living Accommodation

As already detailed, my first night was spent with one of the aircrew teams in their marquee. This was the standard provision for the crews who maintained the aircraft, for in one half of the tent they kept their stores of replacement parts in case of breakdowns, and spares and mechanical tools, and had the space to repair things that could be repaired, using the remainder as their sleeping quarters. They were inevitably a close-knit group, necessary, when it came to servicing the plane and ensuring its safety and airworthiness, working in harmony with each other and understanding each other's skills and interests. Hence it was not appropriate that I should be foisted on to them for more than the one night. The following day I was allotted to join with another small but more disparate group.

Only the aircrew personnel were provided with a store-cum-bedroom marquee but the remainder of the staff had to make the best of whatever materials were available. So, I now moved into a dugout. This was literally a large square hole dug into the ground, somehow or another, I never discovered how, with entrance steps down into it. I assume it was done by hand and must have been a wearisome, strenuous and difficult task. Into this there were the trestle bunks we used as beds where four of us could live and sleep. It sounds horrific, but was probably the best that could be provided in the winter weather. Korea has very cold winters, with temperatures well below freezing and bitter cold winds, so being underground was a wise move. We had one common way, throughout the unit, to keep warm; a heating stove in one corner. The technical experts among us rigged up these works of art, consisting of metal boxed trays, the bottom of which was covered in a layer of sand, and with a chimney. A drum of diesel was stored as near as was safe, and from it a pipe feed, so that a steady drip of diesel was fed onto the sand base and ignited. They must have been made to fairly exacting standards by the mechanics of the unit as people who both understood the theoretical basis for their operation and had a high standard of technical efficiency. Whatever the mechanism, it worked well and we were warm in our dugout. Throughout my stay I was not aware of a problem with any of those we used.

The severity and coldness of the Korean winters can be illustrated by an incident whilst I was still at the Transit Camp in Kure. The Inspector Gunner was called to Korea because of a problem getting the guns to fire at all. He understood it was something to do with the temperature and the call was so insistent that he flew out overnight. He came back steaming and any reference to his visit occasioned some choice oaths about some people who couldn't read a thermometer correctly, not knowing their Fahrenheit from their Centigrade, and ending,

"Forty degrees below, of course the guns couldn't fire at that centigrade temperature!"

It was a clear indication of the severity of the winter weather!

However comfortable we were below ground, it was a different matter outside the dugout. As one who shaved each morning using a safety razor, it was of urgent practical import to me to realise the lengths to which I had to go, in the coldest spells, to shave each morning. Shell or cartridge boxes were readily available and, filled with sand, could serve as heaters as effectively in the open air as did those indoors. We easily had hot water to wash and shave by putting billycans or other containers on the makeshift stoves, and it would soon be boiling away. In normal temperatures, this occasioned no difficulty, as one added cold water or left the hot water to cool, and then used it as it was needed. In the depth of winter, it was a different matter. The trick then was to lather some part of my face, dip the razor into the boiling water and get it to the lathered area as quickly as possible. I had mornings when, in the time it took to raise my shaving brush or razor from the boiling water to my face, the water was cold and almost freezing! On such mornings, the only way was to dispense with any mirror, because any moisture on it would freeze, kneel down as close to the billycan as possible and juggle getting some wetness to one's face at the same time as my razor, and hope to remove some whiskers. It was a painful process! It required spot on timing to avoid either applying water at almost boiling temperature or freezing one's face or fingers. I cannot now imagine why more of us, me included, didn't grow beards!

Eventually, as spring arrived and the weather improved, Peter S and I decided that it would be good if we could have our own accommodation. We approached Jed, our Quartermaster Sergeant, to see what he had available in his store.

"Nothing suitable, for you two,"

was his peremptory answer, thereby showing his judgement as to our practical abilities and his hope that we would go away and leave him in peace. Jed liked his peace! We didn't go away, but pursued our request with further suggestions. As the practical controllers of who used what vehicles, it was up to us to facilitate his requests whenever he wanted to go off on missions to gain something he felt we wanted or to collect allocated materials. We never really understood the nature of his visits, but he couldn't make them unless we could organise a vehicle and driver for him. Power was in our hands –

"OK, so you haven't got anything we could use, but you could surely find us something the next time you go off on one of your missions? You seem able, with your diplomatic skills, to obtain most of the things we need in the unit, so surely you could find some form of tent covering for us as well as some timber so that we could build our own shelter. It's all we'd need."

Not to be outdone, Jed maintained his superior rank and gave himself some room and ability to deal or not with our request, by pouring scorn on the skills of two such simple pen pushers as us to be able to design and erect anything that would do service as a tent!

"Huh, I'm not sure you two have got the skills or strength to build anything!"

"Now don't be like that, Jed, you'd be surprised what we can manage. So, think about it next time you're out."

As well as informal nudges as often as possible, there followed two or three sessions with some threats that we would be unable to find him a vehicle unless he were to come up with the necessary goods for us! As the weeks passed and nothing happened, we thought that he was stringing us along claiming not to have found anything suitable. Whilst privately doubting that he could achieve what we wanted, we kept the pressure on. It worked, and one evening he returned from some mysterious trip and came into the office, saying,

"Come on, you two, I've got something for you to see."

We were both flabbergasted, at least, to see that he had some of the lads dragging a canvas fire hydrant out of the truck he had used that day for his business. These were 3–5 metre circular canvas 'floors', made of layers of canvas stuck together and perhaps one to one and a half inches thick. To these were sown similarly made walls about a metre high. They had been in regular use during the 1939–45 war in areas that were expecting or receiving bombing raids, especially with incendiary bombs, and provided readily available water for the Fire Services. There been one on our road during the war, so I was well aware of their nature. In fact, we now had a dilemma,

"Where in heavens name did you get that? You haven't stolen it or left some place without proper fire safety equipment, have you?"

"Never you mind where it came from. It's probably no longer needed where it was, so I thought of you two!"

Could we manage this thing? Could we even cut it to the shape we wanted? It would provide us with a first class roof, but how did we manufacture walls out of it? Such matters went through both our heads at the same time and we gently tried to demur to Jed,

"Well that's some tent roof, Jed, but it's going to be pretty difficult to do much with it, isn't it? Are you trying to make us look weak and feeble?"

Jed enjoyed our dilemma! He stood surveying us and our discomfiture with some satisfaction, repeating steadily,

"You know that'll keep you dry. There'll not be any water get through that!"

We had to agree. Without losing face, we suggested that this canvas be placed where we would deal with it, whilst we considered our options!

I cannot now recall how we did it – but we did! Without making much of a song and dance about it, we worked out what we could do, and using our own skills and those of the mechanics, who hadn't the attitude of the QMS Jed, we spent a few evenings constructing for ourselves a shelter that was the envy of all. When finished we, naturally, invited QMS Jed to the house warming and grudgingly he had to admit that we had done a fine piece of work, much to his considerable amazement.

"I didn't think you could do it, you know! I really expected that you'd be asking me to take it away again."

We remained very comfortable in our home – and were never wet, nor did our covering canvas skin ever move in the wind!

17. Chief Clerk

I soon discovered the background to my speedy move from Japan to Korea. Apparently, the reservist RA clerk, who had been recalled to duty and sent to administer this unit, had come to the end of his tour of duty and returned to the UK on his due date. The CO had requested a replacement, and a trained clerk from the RASC had been sent and arrived with just a couple of days' delay. The poor unfortunate man had been greeted by the furious ire of the CO, who explained that he already had both RAF and RA personnel, and he wasn't having any RASC person on his unit! All this was expressed somewhat forcibly and the poor man was simply told to clear off. He spent no time with the unit at all, not even to unpack his kitbag! Where he went and what he did remains a mystery.

The CO's anger spread far and wide so that by the time it reached the transit camp in Japan it was virtually a government edict to find an artillery clerk and have him in Korea yesterday! I have no idea what the aristocratic CO made of me. He was pleasant enough to me and we got on well enough during the remainder of his stay, but I have no idea as to what he did with all his apparent anger.

It may well have been that he took steps, unbeknown to me, to obtain an RAF clerk, for a few weeks later, I was joined by Peter S, who was a trained RAF clerk. Between us we managed to administer this almost forgotten unit with some measure of success! Peter knew what had to be done to meet the RAF's requirements – such as the routine daily signals about each of our aircraft's condition and flight worthiness or repair status – so we met these completely.

However, such was, to our eyes, the poorly organised way in which the Korean campaign was conducted that there was no alternative to our doing things our own way, as far as possible.

There was little in the daily routine of the 'office' to cause either of us much concern. The tasks were ones that were well within our capabilities. What became a major side-line of mine followed on from one of the lads saying to me one pay day that his income tax was wrong and he was paying too much.

"Well that's not right," I said, "come and see me in the morning with all the details and I'll see what I can do."

He had the necessary documentation, and it was thus a relatively straightforward matter of contacting the Inland Revenue, making them aware of the situation and getting the repayment of the over payment taken in error. He was naturally delighted with the outcome and I was faced with one after another of the lads sidling up to me and saying his tax was not correct, or his service qualification was not being recognised in his pay. I took each one up and in every case the information given to me proved to be correct, and the error was thus put right.

The upshot was that, on a sunny afternoon some weeks later, three soldiers appeared on site and, on being asked who they were and what they wanted, replied that it was me they wanted to talk to. The conversation went something like this:

"Are you Peter Hutchinson, 7287, the clerk here?"

"Yes."

"We are from the Royal Army Pay Corps, and would like to have a word with you about some of your recent actions."

"I see. What actions in particular?"

"We see from our records that you were in touch with the Inland Revenue about… Is that right?"

"Yes, the Revenue were not aware of his married status and so he was paying too much."

"Yes, so you obtained a rebate for him?"

"Yes, and he was very pleased when he got it."

They then proceeded to fence around about other matters I had dealt with, and I was uncertain what the purpose was, and if in some way I was in trouble. Finally, they said,

"You see, these are normally specialist matters that we deal with and we needed to be sure that everything was in order and being done correctly."

"Oh, I see."

"But you seem to be doing a very good job, and everything seems to be in order. So, all we want to say is well done, and carry on the good work. We only wish all units had someone like you and didn't just leave it all to us."

I relaxed and they departed with good wishes all round, though I failed to see how they would know that something was wrong unless they were told about it, and my Fred's and Joe's had no clue how to even go about contacting them. After all, we normally never saw them.

The one major problem I had to face came when the CO was due to leave and return to the UK sometime in May 1952. Soon into the new year he started to grumble and mutter about the 'war diary'. I knew nothing of the mechanics of such a diary but the CO made it clear that it was his responsibility to provide to the War Office with a daily diary that would log the circumstances of each man's life under his command. Not having completed any day by day diary, he had thus to set about the monumental task of writing this, in long hand, on the special format log that he had.

"Is there any way in which we can help, sir?"

"No, it's my personal responsibility."

"Would it help if I typed it out for you, sir?"

No, we could not help him by typing it. It was his personal responsibility and he would write it in longhand. He did say,

"What you could do would be to give me reminders of significant dates and events."

Not having been aware of this necessity ever arising, I had very little with which to help him. Peter S had other serious questions and priorities entirely, in that he was well aware that the RAF's version of the war diary was an extended version of the 'state of aircraft daily log'. In his terms, it was the RAF's version of the War Diary that was needed. As he explained to me,

"The RAF were in no way interested in the ramblings, written in long hand, long after the event, of a useless Royal Artillery CO!"

Who would be!

"What it needs is proper details of the aircraft, their availability, which one and where they had flown, who had piloted them and what action they had seen and/or taken."

This rumbled on for weeks and weeks. It didn't affect Peter S and myself, for we got on very well, but it meant that Peter S and the CO had never to meet, for there would be ructions, and I could never be certain what the recriminations of an aristocratic RA CO to his RAF clerk might be. It was better for the peace of all that the CO sat at his desk, in his command post lorry, writing away for hour after hour, whilst we simply kept him undisturbed and faced his grumbles!

18. Food

The first evening I arrived, I was invited to partake of a splendid meal, a taster for Christmas itself, and it was amazing fare. In fact, all our food was excellent. Later I was to discover that it was all down to one man, Neddy, our 'Chef', well 'Cook' in those days and situations. He was a man with a chequered history in the forces. Gradually I began to discover that he had served in all three services and been promoted and demoted more times than he could remember for, euphemistically, he enjoyed a drink! Indeed, he had a major drink problem and would occasionally be 'hors de combat' on his bed for a few days, but never in our experience when he was required.

Amazingly he always saw that we were fed sumptuously. His methodology followed the same pattern, in that every few weeks he would arrive in the office and say,

"I need a truck."

Until I began to understand his way of operating, I might not be switched on enough, and ask,

"What do you want it for? Will a Jeep do or a 15cwt?"

And I would get some vague reply, such as,

"I've got some business to do!" or, "If we're going to eat next week, I've got to do some business."

Once I understood that our supplies of food from the UK largely consisted of sacks of oatmeal, flour, potatoes or similar stodgy and boring, if basic, foodstuff, the nature of his mysterious trips became clear. In Neddy's terms, all that stuff needed changing for something better. So, I never questioned his requests again and, subject to the demands on our limited transport, would make the necessary three-tonne truck available, with driver, as soon as it was possible. The difficulty was that no one was ever aware of how long the said truck, driver and cook would be away for – one day, two or even a week. So, I found myself seeking to avoid awkward questions, and when necessary, offering vague answers, even lies, to anyone who did not need to know.

Having got the truck, Neddy would then load it with the surplus boring provisions we could manage without and set off for the American camps. What took place there, what relationships were built up over the months or what drinking together ensued can only be imagined, for it was a strict secret between Neddy and the driver who went with him. Neddy was particularly concerned to be allocated the driver who would be able to fraternise with his contacts and keep his mouth shut when he returned to camp. Eventually they would arrive back with that selfsame truck loaded with chickens, meats, vegetables, fruit and every other food that I could imagine, and in plentiful quantities! All bartered from the American cooks! Neddy always assured me that it was not a one-sided bargain, for the US cooks were short of the very basic food we had and were glad to make the exchange. It was from this combination that he would produce the most exquisite meals that we ate day after day.

Before I arrived, he had built his own oven. A 50-gallon oil drum sat outside and through a feed tube dripped oil on to a flat bed of sand over which the oven stood. It was a system that worked well. Perhaps a trip to some engineer outfit had enabled its construction! We also had an assistant cook, and on one occasion, when Neddy seemed to have been away for a few days, I took the opportunity to talk with him;

"You seem to manage pretty well when Neddy isn't here. Does it work OK for you as well? How do you manage it all?"

His reply was very interesting and showed a lot about the essential humanity of promoted-demoted Cook in all three services.

"I've been well trained, Peter, by Neddy! That man's taught me everything I know. OK, I was taught the basic things about cooking in the RAF school, but, I can tell you, it didn't deal with things like we have here. You know there was a section of the course about cooking in conditions like this, and we used to have to go to the far end of the field, behind some old unused hangars and be told to get creative and find something on which we could cook. But, Peter, dozens of previous courses had done the same exercises and, if you looked around, there was everything you needed – bricks, metal grills, everything, so it was so easy to set something up and prepare a meal. You know if the weather was bad, rather than go out in the wet and mud, they'd allow us to do it all in the hangars! I ask you! You know other units don't have ovens like we have, nor the food that we have. It's all down to Neddy, he's brilliant! I've not met another cook in the RAF that can touch him. I'll tell you, he's taught me all I really know. And all I can say is, it would be God help you lot if all you'd only got was me as they sent me out from training school. You'd all be hungry!"

The training that Neddy gave applied not only to his assistant but to the Korean orphans, displaced and homeless, that he took in. One of the unknown aspects of life there, and it passed by almost all of us, was the number of Koreans, displaced by the war and the devastation of the countryside, who had nothing and nowhere to go, so hung around our camps. The official orders were that we should not fraternise in any way but to be on our guard at all times, for any one of these apparently innocent Koreans could be an infiltrator, fifth columnist or North Korean agent. How would we be able to judge? We couldn't! Naturally, the youngsters would gravitate to the kitchen area in the hope of begging some food, and Neddy would have some personal way of communicating, no doubt with signs, and of assessing them. Some he would send away but two or three were allowed to stay. As his assistant said, in the above conversation,

"You know, he trains those Korean kids. They're not allowed in the kitchen or near your food until they are capable."

"Yes, I notice that sometimes they are on their own at breakfast time and they cook all the food."

"That's just what I mean. Until they can take an egg in each hand, break it cleanly into the frying pan and know when it's cooked as you want it, they are not allowed in the kitchen. That's how careful he is – and good with them. I don't have any trouble from them at all."

It wasn't just the basic every day meals which were a substantial proficiency of Neddy and his team, for when the officers decided to invite all the most senior officers from HQ for afternoon tea, I have rarely seen such a display of delicious looking, light pastries, mouth-wateringly laid out on a set of tables prior to the bigwigs' arrival. Because of the distance rigidly kept between the officers and other ranks, even though I was chief clerk I knew little of the nature of this event until I saw this display, brought into one end of our office as a staging post before it went to be laid out in the officer's mess.

"Neddy, what's all this about?"

I asked.

"Oh, didn't you know? The top brass are coming in about half an hour."

"Yes."

"And I've had to prepare afternoon tea for them. So, you can imagine our Right Honourable CO gave the strictest instructions as to the hors'd'ouevre, the slimmest sandwiches and the translucent pastries he wanted. So here it is!"

The next day I had the temerity to ask the CO if all had gone well the previous afternoon, and, for once, he replied with some fulsome praise,

"Very well thank you, Hutchinson, and Cook laid out a splendid array for us. It went down very well with our guests. Much appreciated it was."

I passed the message on to Neddy, not knowing whether the CO would have bothered. It was part of the skill of Neddy that, without any disruption to our normal eating, it was all provided as if it was a normal part of everyday life.

His passion for food never diminished and when he heard that a

"Small Indian Ambulance unit,"

in his phrase – though, in fact, it was a large hospital unit – had arrived on the peninsula, he was soon standing in the office asking for a Jeep,

"For a few days."

Unusually he wanted to drive it himself, perhaps because it was over a fortnight later when he returned!

"How've you got on?"

I asked him, and he replied,

"Oh, them poor buggers, they've got now't you know. I thought our stuff was pretty basic and minimal, but they've nothing. But it was great to be with the Indian cooks and watch how they use their spices and what goes with what and for what purposes. It's not to make the food hot, but to flavour it delicately,"

he explained.

"But the only trouble was they have so little supplies, so I could only beg very tiny amounts of spices from them."

Nevertheless, from these ingredients he produced the best curries that I can still remember 60 years later.

As I write, I read of the British troops in Afghanistan rearing a pet turkey, which they hope and intend to eat on Christmas Day. I hope they have a cook of the quality of Neddy to do this special turkey and the soldier eaters proud. Neddy! The best drunk I ever met. Cheers to his memory.

19. The Church and Its Chaplains

The church, as an integral part of army life, has hardly figured in this story so far, for only when I arrived in Kure, Japan, did I find a chaplain and a church with a regular congregation and life. The two were not related, for the church was part of an Australian families' living quarters' provision.

For me, this separation of army life and the church changed once I arrived in Korea as I met and was helped by a very great Methodist chaplain, Revd Bill. Throughout this account I have been gently, even satirically, critical of the army's organisation. Some of that was inevitable because communication with basic grade serving soldiers was not then seen as anything to be considered or undertaken, so things happened without our being aware of their mechanics, only sometimes their results.

This was no doubt the case with my sudden move to Korea, for I presume the chaplain for whom I had been technically 'working' must have made enquiries when I failed to turn up morning after morning! I assume that, through the chaplain's department communications system, he must have informed the Revd Bill who was, at that time, the only Methodist chaplain in Korea. So, one afternoon, he arrived at the unit and presented himself to me, the first of a number of similar meetings in which he provided me with help and guidance, and the opportunity to talk of some things that otherwise lay hidden deep inside myself. I was a candidate for the ministry and he asked about my reading and preparation for the examinations I had to take. When the time came, he arranged for and conducted my oral examination, with another chaplain present, and informed the church authorities accordingly. I remember it well, and am still ashamed of my failure to understand and be able to answer some of the questions, even after his gentle prodding help!

As I came over the months to know him, I also became the recipient of some of the aspects of his daily, normal life that, I suspect, would otherwise have been kept to himself. Whilst we were technically in a period without active warfare, negotiations were ongoing in Panmunjom, and, on clear nights, we could see the searchlights shining in the distance indicating that the talks were still continuing. So, two sets of troops were 'settled' behind a 'no man's land' that separated them, kept them apart and apparently maintained a fiction of no action. The reality was that there was nightly activity, even if the activity during the daylight hours was very limited. Revd Bill was attached to an infantry regiment and so would travel day after day into the dugouts, trenches or gun emplacements to visit his 'flock'. There were days when he travelled on to see me after such visits, and sometimes when he arrived visibly shaken because, on a visit to some look-out or dugout that had been discovered by the North Korean troops, they were shelled, often with precise accuracy. So, his visit had been undertaken with gunfire all around and shells bursting close at hand.

On other occasions, he was clearly dead beat tired and, slowly, I pieced together something of his nightly activity. Patrols were sent out into the so called demilitarised zone every night, and their CO would not retire until he knew every patrol and man had returned safe and sound. Revd Bill stayed with him. I understood they played a deal of chess! The horrendous occasions were, of course, when all or some of a patrol did not return because they had met opposition or an ambush, for the opposing force also sent out nightly patrols, attempting to infiltrate 'our' lines, we believed. On such occasions, depending on the circumstances, it was not unknown for Revd Bill to go out, crawling into the 'no man's land territory', to find some 'lost' soldier, even dragging some injured man back, in the hope of keeping him alive. Inevitably in some cases he would minister to a dying man. It was so easy to imagine that senior officers were, and still are, well protected from the day to day hours of active war, but here was a glimpse of one such officer, wearily waiting night after night for the safe return of his six to eight men patrols, and the spiritual guide who supported him every night.

Elsewhere I recall the death of one of our pilots, Jo (Bryan) Luscombe, a shock and a loss readily felt by all in the unit, and a couple of days later, at the 'door' of the office tent, there stood Revd Bill with a face and demeanour that so clearly spoke of pain, sadness, grief saying,

"Peter, can you spare the time to come with me. I've got a duty to perform and would appreciate your help, if it can be managed."

As I replied,

"Yes,"

and went towards him, he led me outside and away from others to say,

"Someone has to lay Capt. Luscombe to rest and send his body home."

Once again, I knew nothing of the background activity. As chief clerk, the only task I had undertaken was to report Jo Luscombe's death in the daily signal to the War Office. I had not informed anyone else, though I knew we had arranged for his body to be collected from his plane, but arrangements to take his body to any mortuary or resting place, inform any family, or arrange for any transport of his body back to Australia had not been my responsibility. But somehow those wheels ground on, even though the so called chief clerk knew and did nothing about them. No doubt our self-contained CO had played his part. This, alas, indicates that my knowledge and information was very partial because many wheels ground on without there being any need to keep little me informed! Thus Revd Bill and I, almost overwhelmed by our own grief, drove to some airport, I know not where, for it seemed to be in the middle of nowhere. There we committed Jo's remains, in a coffin draped with the Australian flag, and his family to the peace and care of God Almighty. Such is one part of the life of a forces' chaplain. Only later, online, did I discover that Jo had a wife and family in Australia to which his body was returned, and where it was given a hero's burial, tributes and continuing honour.

1903 Flight's camp lay close by Divisional HQ where there was a church and a 'resident' senior chaplain. It was the natural place for me to worship and I did so Sunday by Sunday with regularity. I know that because, returning one pleasant sunny Sunday morning, I was accosted by one of our officers, sitting relaxing outside their tent,

"Ah, Hutchinson, been to church again, have you?"

"Yes, sir."

"You know, it's a good job you go to church each week, for it's the only way I know that it's Sunday. So, I'm very grateful to you. Tell me it must be near Easter, is it?"

"Yes, sir, it happens to be next Sunday."

"Oh, thanks for that. I don't like missing Easter."

It was, however, a bleak experience for me, both on Sunday mornings and also on Wednesday when there was an early Holy Communion service. There were not many in the congregation each Sunday and literally only one or two of us each Wednesday – the other person then being a Church Army Evangelist with a roving commission but a base at HQ.

Together we shared our feelings, much worse for him than me, about the senior chaplain, who was his colleague. The chaplain's location on a map of church distinctiveness would be 'high Anglican' and, as I later discovered was common at that time, such senior men were similar to the aristocrats of society at large – hardly noticing lesser mortals, and when they did only with clear condescension, be they 'evangelical' or merely 'lay'. On Wednesday mornings, he would proceed through the Eucharist until the point where the bread and wine are distributed to those present, and there he would give us both a look that dared us to go forward, and as quickly as possible proceeded with the service. It was a most distressing experience for us both, mere laymen, who had dedicated their lives to serve the same Jesus Christ. Every sinew of my Christian being rejects every nuance that lies behind that chaplain's way, but there was never opportunity to say so, because he didn't stay around long enough to be spoken to, and I had to think of the implications for his Church Army colleague, who probably met it from many others day by day. Such were the hierarchies and powers that were common in the army, and probably the wider society of that day, and has, to some extent, been ameliorated in the following decades.

20. Rest and Recuperation

Seoul railway station as it was in 1951
[Thanks to Page F30]

In every theatre of war, it is, if at all possible, planned for there to be some time away from the stresses of combat so that soldiers can relax. In the Korean war, the inbuilt relaxation was a five-day break back in Japan.

It's not that easy to ensure that all things always are done properly. So much, in my experience of national service, was haphazard and disorganised. This was shown, for example, when it became the turn of myself and another lad to have five days Rest and Recuperation [R & R] in Tokyo in the spring. We left our unit and travelled in a truck to

Seoul and the Transit Camp. We spent one night there, and it proved to be as awful as was the general consensus told to me when I had arrived in Korea. Next morning all who were due to go on R & R were taken to the airport, only to discover that Commonwealth troops were flown to Tokyo as a grace and favour arrangement with the US Airforce. There was not enough room for any but a few of us that day. In this pitiful condition, with five days break in imagined luxury disappearing before our eyes, we watched USA staff walk onto the aircraft. Kindly, we were informed by the NCO in charge,

"Look, I'm sorry, lads, but there's nothing I can do about it. I'll have to take you back to the Camp until we try again tomorrow. I know it's pretty crap, but all I can do is give you a couple of hours, and there's the Yank's PX, so go and get a cup of tea and relax until I get you all back here."

I said to my companion 'B' that I thought that was very unsatisfactory, but I had an idea. So, would he come with me and not go to the PX? He agreed and we walked right to the far edge of the airport where there was a small Air Traffic Control office. When any of our aircraft needed to be in Seoul, perhaps to pick up spare parts, I would ring the folk in this office and make the arrangements with them, so I 'knew' them. I knocked on the door and entered,

"Hello, I'm Peter Hutchinson from the Air OP Flight and make the links with you when any of our Austers have to come here,"

was my opening. Greetings over and an obviously a friendly reception, I went on to explain our problem that there were not enough seats for us on the R & R plane, and I was wondering if there might be any seats available on the daily Courier Flight? Somehow, I knew this left at 4pm each day to Tokyo. They checked, and there was no problem, we could certainly have seats. As long as we were in the right spot to board, all would be well. When all the others had returned to the Transit Camp, we went to the PX and then caught the Courier, accompanied by more US officers in clean, shiny, posh uniforms that looked as if they had come from a shop that morning. In addition, many carried garment hangars with their civilian clothes inside! In our unsmart uniforms and without any civilian suits, we felt envious, for they seemed to inhabit a different world from ours!

Arriving in Tokyo, there was consternation, it was May Day and there were riots against the control of Japan by the American forces. We were hurried on to buses, told to crouch down so we were not seen and the buses looked empty, and, in this fashion, we were taken to the R & R centre. During the day, other buses had been shot at but we were not.

The time in Tokyo was an amazing experience for us both. The city itself was, then, a mixture of modern skyscraper buildings crowded together and all mixed in with the ancient emperor's palaces and beautiful gardens. There was so much to see. But we were in a centre on the outskirts of the city and needed to travel into the centre by train. We both had some experience of the London Tube and its rush hour crowds, but they were nothing compared with Tokyo commuter trains. Whatever time of day we travelled, it seemed to be the same, and there were station staff whose only job appeared to be literally to push passengers into each compartment. That was small inconvenience for a never to be forgotten experience. Exploring the shops was similarly exciting and as I had only recently turned 21 so had some birthday money and bought a Rolex watch and a Japanese made camera. When our photographer saw some of the photos I took, he asked to see the camera and confirmed that it had a very high-quality lens.

Almost all the British troops on R & R at the time had travelled from Pusan, on the southern tip of Korea, but we did not know that. On our arrival, we were processed, had our five days R & R, and then saw our details on the movement orders. We were down to fly to Pusan, and my protestations to the Warrant Officer in charge received short shrift,

"Don't know about that. You came in with the lot from Pusan, and you'll go out with them. That's my responsibility, and you'll have to sort out what you do about it."

We did. At the Pusan Transit Camp, much, much better than Seoul, we made arrangements to be taken by train to Seoul, though we had to wait 24 hours. That journey was another eye opener, with armed guards on every coach and on most bridges that we crossed or went under, all because of possible attacks from Northern Korean infiltrators. The countryside was beautiful but devastated by the war, that had been going for three years or so, and looked in a barren pitiable state. At Seoul, it was back to the Transit Camp and once again negotiating a lift in a lorry going our way. Next morning, after arriving back in camp, the CO called me into his office to explain how and why my five days R & R had taken eight days! I explained, and he grudgingly, I felt, said that under the circumstances he would take no further action. I was prepared to argue with him, for I would have wanted to point out that we might have waited two to three extra days in Seoul Transit Camp for a plane to take us to Tokyo.

21. A New CO

As spring turned into summer, we were faced with a very different commander. He was a man who knew what he was about and had considerable experience, most recently in Malaya. As soon as he arrived, he started to move around, visiting every part of the camp and all its personnel, take control and see if changes were necessary. Almost ten days went by whilst the two Peters were unsuccessfully trying to have a session with him, acquaint him with the nature of the unit and deal with matters that were pending. He clearly avoided meeting with us until he finally said,

"I want a session with you two tomorrow morning. OK?"

At last, we felt we might share some of our burden with the new boss. We got a surprise. It was a beautiful sunny morning, so the new CO suggested we sat outside and, as it happened, well away from anyone else.

"Right," he said, "now that we're together, I want to know what's really going on in this place with you two."

Somewhat puzzled and having little idea what lay behind his questioning, we fenced around with each other for quite some time until eventually he said,

"Look, you two have a reputation all across the Far East command, and I'm trying to find out how it is that you've got that reputation and power."

We had little idea as to what he was referring, but slowly matters began to unravel and we were asked to explain.

How, he asked, had we come to have a brand new photographic vehicle provided to us direct from the War Office? We explained that we had a first rate photographer on the unit. He knew! He was, we explained, another reservist recalled to duty, and he had a professional business in the UK and a reputation to try to preserve. It was, as he knew, also a crucial part of our job as a unit to take photographs across the 38th parallel. Our photographer had submitted many of the photographs taken on the unit to such as the Illustrated London News, the photographic acme of such weekly journals, where some were printed, and for others there were letters from the editor explaining the reasons why he had been unable to print them. Thus, when our photographer outlined to us that there was a new all singing and dancing photographic truck fitted with dark room and full of wonderful equipment and how he would love to have one to use, we felt it was our job, and duty, to get one, so we sat down and constructed a signal indenting for one, making out the case for such to be ours, and also decided that, unless it was sent direct to the War Office, it would get nowhere. So that is where we sent it – and, yes, we too, were very surprised and pleased that within a very short time it arrived. The only trouble was that we had not realised that it needed a generator and we had to indent for one of those too!

"And did you discuss all this with the CO before you did that?"

Sheepishly we had to reply,

"Well, no, sir, it didn't seem necessary."

How, he asked, had he heard that the specialist Pay Corps had recently paid us a visit and said that they had never previously met with such as us? We explained that the circumstances of our being in Korea had meant that some of the men's finances were not in order, and I had felt it was our duty to set about sorting it out. Yes, the Pay Corps had visited, to check our records, they said, and see that they were all correct. We were relieved when they found everything to be correct.

This interrogation went on for a couple of hours, with our new CO visibly relaxing before our eyes and finally laughing. Explaining that he had been concerned that he might be facing two trouble makers, and that we were the reason for spending ten days getting to know the unit, and us, before he confronted us, he was chuffed to know the truth. So, had we been a nuisance? Did it mean that we must change? Did he have new orders for us as to how to behave?

"No, no,"

he laughed,

"you've got reputations right across the far East and, as far as I'm concerned, carry on the way you are. You've done a brilliant job. Don't stop! But in future I expect you to keep me informed about what you're doing!"

Only one incident, previously touched upon, marred life in 1903 Air OP Flight for the remainder of that summer. It happened on the 5th June, a bright sunny afternoon, when the radio operators, who worked from a small 'station' next to my desk, started to speak in agitated tones.

"We've lost him,"

to be followed by advice as to steps to take to retrieve the situation. And relieved,

"He's back,"

or,

"Got him!"

Radio signals were not always on target or easy to pick up, so that sort of conversation was not too unusual. But on this occasion the voices remained concerned for,

"He's on his way home. He should be nearly here."

And,

"Something's not right. He's in trouble."

Peter S, I and others were soon outside scanning the sky for sight of that little Auster aircraft with Captain Bryan (Jo to us) Luscombe at the controls. All seemed well, he was aligned correctly for the airstrip, and seemed to be making a perfect landing as he slowly approached and lost height. Then, almost at the start of the runway, the plane veered to its right, still losing height, left the runway approach, crossed the river and crashed into the hillside opposite. Every man of the Flight, who was aware of what was happening, was in and across the water in minutes and scrambling up the steep rough wooded bank towards the aircraft. Those of us who were not in the nearest group were suddenly stopped in our tracks,

"It's too late. He's dead. Go back. We need to examine what's happened here. The rest of you can't help now."

Before the day was out the results of that examination were out, Jo had been shot at and had received a bullet in his back, which must have knocked him out, or at the very least given him considerable pain. As matters became clearer, the pilots began to make sense of what must have happened, and could explain that Jo had probably passed out, returned to consciousness and had fought to bring his aircraft and himself back to safety. Only as he arrived over the runway approach had he died.

Succeeding research has shown that it was typical of the man. An Australian, he had attended Hale School, where he was in the Rugby first XV, Captain of the cricket XI and a prefect, and, as one of his team members wrote, 'Everybody that knew him firmly believed the sun shone out of him.' He was the Australian Army's first aviation battle casualty since the 1939–45 war. Through his sister's work and donation, an Air OP display has been created by the Royal Australian Artillery Historical Company, to honour Jo (Captain Bryan) and others.

The succeeding weeks were pleasant in that the weather was fine, dry and warm. We now had a boss in whom Peter S and I had confidence. We could swim in the afternoons, if there was time. But of much greater significance was the date of departure for home that was quickly approaching.

22. Coming Home

At last, the day came to leave. We had to travel to Pusan, where the main transit camp was located. It was a repeat process, in reverse, of the preparations for coming to Korea, including one night in the dreaded Seoul transit camp. All our clothes had to be handed in and new ones taken, so that there was no chance, we were told, that we would carry any infections home that way. We had to be injected with this and that. Spotting the medical orderly who had given me the injections at the dentists, I joined his queue. His technique hadn't changed and the statement,

"Two smart taps, and the job's done,"

was repeated and, of course, the process was painless.

Then it was getting on the boat, finding that we were allocated hammocks in a lower deck, but, praise be, we could sleep on deck. We did that right until the end of the journey when we arrived at Liverpool.

As on the outward journey, we stopped and picked up returning army personnel in Hong Kong, Singapore and Colombo, but there was only chance to explore Hong Kong, which it was good to do.

Arriving at Liverpool in stormy weather, those of us from Korea were surprised to find that we were given more than a quick examination by customs. Friends who had returned before us had reported, especially if the Korean contingent was the major one on board, that they were virtually exempt from examination, but not so for us. My bags had to emptied for them to be examined, and the customs officers disregarded any comment such as,

"I've just come from Korea, what chance do you think we've had to bring anything back that we shouldn't have?"

From Lime Street Station, it was a train to Woolwich to go through an extended Pusan sorting out experience. We arrived there on Thursday morning, and that was the day of our release for many of the National Servicemen, me included. We were told that we could not expect to be discharged at least until Friday and maybe even later. However, I found myself called out to move from this examination to the next, and by late afternoon I had finished and was furnished with my travel warrant to get me to Shrewsbury. Only at the end of it all did I recall that the assurance of the War Office to the Methodist Church had been that I could legally be sent to Korea because I would be discharged on Thursday 28th August 1952, which met the legal requirement that I would have five days before the start of the College term. They knew, and remembered and kept it, but who they were and by what mechanism they understood I, only a simple ignorant gunner, had no need or right to know.

Postscript

I apologise that to recount the significance of that last phase I shall need to explain in some detail the rules of the Methodist Church as they applied in the late 1940s to the mid-1950s. Some years after my National Service and consequent entering into training at theological college for ordination into the Methodist ministry I met the Revd S at a church gathering. He had been the superintendent minister of the circuit where my father had served and we had lived during my 6th Form years. As he met me he said,

"Peter, I am glad you're here and we've met because I very much want to talk to you and apologise."

My reply was one of puzzlement, to which he continued,

"When I was your Super and you were starting to preach and taking steps to becoming a minister, I never met you and talked with you as I should have done. That was wrong of me, but I trusted your father, who was such a competent colleague, and I just assumed that he would deal with all the things that were necessary. It could have been so different for you if I had done what I should have done, and I can only say how much I regret that and want you to know and to apologise to you."

To tease out the significance of that much longer conversation, I need to make an excursion into Methodism's then rules. These stated that to candidate for the ministry of the church, men needed, by the time one's candidature was accepted, to be an approved Local Preacher, and secondly to have completed one's National Service. A further significant rule was that candidates were not allowed to marry until they were ordained seven years after acceptance and starting training. That implied three years in college and four years of practical training as a probationer in a circuit.

These two conditions for candidates I implicitly accepted, and they structured my candidature. What the Revd S was indicating was that there was a way round the second of those rules. If I had gone to university – and the course of study would have been irrelevant – as was normal for all university students, my National Service would have been delayed until I completed my studies. Then in my second year, had I candidated and been accepted, I would automatically have been given permission by the church to complete the degree. That year would have been included as one of the seven years prior to ordination, and the length of that time would even have been reduced to six years, possibly two in college and four in a probationer appointment. Also, once in this process, my National Service would have been delayed, as all probationer ministers were excused such service.

To explain the timescales of these two routes, they would have operated for me as follows. In the route, I took, from 1950 to 1952 I did my National Service, from 1952 to 1955 was spent at college, and then from 1955 to 1959 serving as a probationer prior to ordination and being allowed to marry. The route Revd S suggested would have been to study at university between 1950 and 1953, be accepted as a candidate for ministry in 1952, followed by five years of study and training, culminating in ordination in 1957, and being allowed to marry – all without doing National Service. In fact, the rules changed during the early 1950s, making the timescales different, so that I was allowed to marry my fiancée 1956, but not altering the fact that, had I chosen to go to university, I would never have,

"Wasted two years doing National Service,"

in Revd S's phrase.

That raised, and still raises, for me the question of the value, or otherwise, that I put on my two years' experiences of National Service. None of that early demeaning and dehumanising behaviour, no wasted hours 'square bashing', no being pushed to apply to be an officer and face WOSB when I had no interest in it, no training to be Technical Assistant but never actually being tested, thus qualified and paid accordingly, no possibility of going to the School of Artillery blazing a trail, no messing around in a transit camp in Japan for three plus months, nor spending eight months in the awful Korean conditions. Quite a lot on that side of the scales. On the other I wouldn't have lived with men of a very different background from mine, who came to accept my difference and respect me – if only for my helping them to bed when they had too much to drink! No meeting with public schoolboys, and some with inflated ideas of their social status and ability to control and order 'lesser mortals' like me and come, not to admire them, but to accept them – and get on with them as equals. No coming to understand the mechanisms of a vast organisation that had its separate ways of dealing with this bit and that bit, so that their major resource, their people like me, could not and would not be considered or taken account of as individuals. No consideration of, and having the possibility of, the certainty I felt, that I would be killed and thus coming to terms with death as an inevitability. No foreign travel to the Far East and seeing glimpses of countries and peoples that I might never have seen. No coming to understand that every other country was not peopled by unwashed, starving people who needed 'saving'. No dawn vision of Japanese islands 'floating' in the bluest, blue sea I have ever seen, and still recall. No meeting with the Japanese girl at the church choir, and hearing from her some of the practical details and horrendous implications for the people from Hiroshima on whom the first atomic bomb dropped, such as trying to walk or crawl miles with burnt flesh and skin hanging off. Such is our inhumanity. No meeting with Japanese people and being left with the conundrum as to how and why such a charming, gentle people could produce people who could and did commit the most terrible atrocities to others, particularly the Korean people.

On balance, I feel I am a better person for the experience!